Tim Price

The Radicalisation of Bradley Manning

Bloomsbury Methuen Drama

An imprint of Bloomsbury Publishing Plc

50 Bedford Square	1385 Broadway
London	New York
WC1B 3DP	NY 10018
UK	USA

www.bloomsbury.com

Bloomsbury is a registered trade mark of Bloomsbury Publishing Plc

First published 2012
Reprinted 2013

British Library Cataloguing-in-Publication Data
A catalogue record for this book is available from the British Library.

ISBN: PB:	978-1-4081-7287-2
EPDF:	978-1-4081-7289-6
EPUB:	978-1-4081-7288-9

Library of Congress Cataloging-in-Publication Data
A catalog record for this book is available from the Library of Congress.

Typeset by Country Setting, Kingsdown, Kent

The Radicalisation of Bradley Manning

by

Tim Price

First performed on 12 April 2012
at Tasker Milward V C School, Haverfordwest

NATIONAL

THEATRE

WALES

The Radicalisation of Bradley Manning
was commissioned and produced by National Theatre Wales.
It was first performed on 12 April 2012 at Tasker Milward V C
School, Haverfordwest, as part of National Theatre Wales'
second year of work.

The production then toured to Cardiff High School
and Connah's Quay High School, Flintshire.

CAST

Matthew Aubrey
Harry Ferrier
Gwawr Loader
Kyle Rees
Anjana Vasan
Sion Daniel Young

CREATIVE TEAM

Writer	**Tim Price**
Director	**John E McGrath**
Designer	**Chloe Lamford**
Lighting Designer	**Natasha Chivers**
Sound Designer	**Mike Beer**
Multi-Platform Designer	**Tom Beardshaw**
Emerging Director	**James Doyle-Roberts**

Producer	**Lucy Davies**
Assistant Producer	**Michael Salmon**
Production Manager	**David Evans**
Technical Stage Manager	**Jacob Gough**
Company Stage Manager	**Fiona Curtis**
Deputy Stage Manager	**Gemma Thomas**
Costume Supervisor and Wardrobe Mistress	**Jo Nicholls**
Production Technician	**Matt Gibson**
AV	**Dan Trenchard**
Promoter	**Catherine Paskell**
Choreographer	**Kylie-Ann Smith**
Vocal Coach	**Simon Reeves**
Military Advisor	**Jolyon 'JJ' Walker**
Rehearsal Assistant	**Richard Lakos**
Rehearsal Technical Assistant	**Rhodri Hunt**

National Theatre Wales

was launched in November 2009,
and creates invigorating theatre in the English language,
rooted in Wales, with an international reach. By April 2012,
it had staged 17 productions in locations all over Wales,
at the Edinburgh Festival Fringe and the London International
Mime Festival. In October 2011, National Theatre Wales
was described as 'one of the best things to happen
to the stage in the past five years' by the *Observer*.

For more information, visit: nationaltheatrewales.org

Past productions include: *A Good Night Out in the Valleys*;
The Devil Inside Him; *Love Steals Us from Loneliness*;
The Persians (winner of the Ted Hughes Award for Poetry and TMA
Award for Best Design); *The Passion* – 'one of the outstanding
theatrical events not only of this year, but of the decade'
(*Observer*) – and *The Village Social*.

National Theatre Wales is supported by
Arts Council of Wales and the Welsh Government.

National Theatre Wales
30 Castle Arcade
Cardiff / CF10 1BW

Phone +44 (0)29 2035 3070
info@nationaltheatrewales.org
nationaltheatrewales.org

Twitter: @ntwtweets

Cyngor Celfyddydau Cymru
Arts Council of Wales

Noddir gan
Lywodraeth Cymru
Sponsored by
Welsh Government

NATIONAL THEATRE WALES

Cast

Matthew Aubrey trained at the Royal Welsh College of Music and Drama.

Theatre credits include: *The Passion* (National Theatre Wales & WildWorks); *War Horse* (National Theatre); *Thoroughly Modern Millie* and *Love's Labour's Lost* (RWCMD).

Television credits include: *Privates* (Twenty Twenty Television for BBC), *Birdsong* (WTTV), *Gracie* (BBC), *Framed* (BBC) and *Sinking of Laconia* (Talkback Thames/Teamworx).

Film credits include: *Dagenham Girls* (Number 9 Films), *The Gospel of Us* (Rondo Media). Radio credits include: *Lemon Meringue Pie* (BBC Radio 4).

Harry Ferrier trained at Royal Academy of Dramatic Art.

Theatre credits include: *Caravaggio's Head* and *After the Storm* (Both Sgript Cymru).

Television credits include: *The Silence, Monroe, Dr. Who* and *Young Dracula* (BBC); and *I Shouldn't Be Alive* (Discovery Channel).

Film credits include: *House of Boys* (De Lux Productions), *Nightwatching* (Kassander Productions), *Flick* (Monster Films) and *Calorie* (Screen Academy Wales).

Gwawr Loader trained at the Royal Welsh College of Music and Drama (RWCMD).

Theatre credits include: *My People* (development workshop) (National Theatre Wales); *Much Ado About Nothing* (Mappa Mundi); *King Lear* (RWCMD); *In The Blood* (RWCMD); *The Magical Myths of the Mabinogi* (National Youth Theatre of Wales); *Cafe Cariad* (National Youth Theatre of Wales); *The Merchant of Venice* (National Youth Theatre of Great Britain).

Television credits include: *Uned 5* (Antena). Radio credits include: *The Verb: The Tempest / Y Storm* extract (BBC Radio 3;) *Losing Louis* (RWCMD); *Other Hands* (RWCMD); Winner of the Hobsons Prize.

Kyle Rees trained at the Royal Scottish Academy of Music & Drama.

Theatre credits include: *The Passion* (National Theatre Wales/WildWorks), *Three Sisters, Black Snow, Romeo & Juliet, A Midsummer's Night Dream, The American Clock, Hedda Gabler, Les Miserables, Blood Wedding, Seussical the Musical, My Fair Lady, West Side Story*, and *Sir, No Sir!*

Television credits include: *The Indian Doctor* (BBC), *Emmerdale* (ITV), *The Cut (BBC), Hollyoaks* and *Hollyoaks Later* (Lime Pictures), Y Pris (S4C).

Film credits include: *The Gospel of Us* (Rondo Media/Film Agency for Wales) and *The Spa*.

Anjana Vasan trained at at the Royal Welsh College of Music and Drama.

Theatre credits include: *In the Blood and The Stone* (RWCMD).

Television credits include: *Fresh Meat* (Channel 4) and *Asia at War: Fighting for India* (The History Channel).

Radio credits include: *The Rules-66 Books* (Bush Theatre).

Sion Daniel Young trained at the Royal Scottish Academy of Music & Drama.

Theatre credits include: *House of America* (Theatr Genedlaethol Cymru), *Llwyth* (*Tribe*) (Sherman Cymru) and *Titus* (Imaginate Festival).

Television credits include: *Casualty* (BBC), *Tissues and Issues* (BBC Wales), *Hotel Eddie* (S4C).

Film credits include: P*rivate Peaceful, Daisy Chain, The Street.*

Radio credits include: *The Dolls Tea Set* (BBC Radio 4) and *Hoshiko* (BBC Radio).

Creative Team

Tim Price   Writer

Tim Price's theatre credits include: *For Once* (Pentabus, Hampstead Theatre and national tour) *Salt Root and Roe* (Donmar Warehouse, Trafalgar Studios), *Demos* (Traverse Theatre) *Will and George* shortlisted for the Verity Bargate *Award 2011, and* Café Cariad (National Youth Theatre of Wales). The Donmar Warehouse has been nominated for the Olivier Award for Outstanding Achievement in an Affiliate Theatre for *Salt Root and Roe.*

John E McGrath   Director

John E McGrath is Artistic Director of National Theatre Wales. Previously Artistic Director of Contact Theatre, Manchester, John trained in New York, where he was also Associate Director of Mabou Mines. In 2005, he was awarded the NESTA Cultural Leadership Award. He directed National Theatre Wales' inaugural production, *A Good Night Out In The Valleys,* in March 2010, and *Love Steals Us from Loneliness* in October 2010.

Chloe Lamford   Designer

Chloe's designs for theatre include: *Salt, Root and Roe* (Donmar Warehouse), *Disco Pigs and Sus* (Young Vic), *Knives In Hens, An Appointment With The Wicker Man* (National Theatre of Scotland); *The Gate Keeper* (Manchester Royal Exchange), *Ghost Story* (Sky Arts Live Drama), *Britannicus* (Wilton's Music Hall), *My Romantic History* (Crucible, Sheffield/ Bush), *Joseph K, The Kreutzer Sonata* (Gate), *Songs from a Hotel Bedroom* (Linbury Studio ROH + Tour), *It Felt Empty When the Heart Went at First But It Is Alright Now* (Clean Break, installation at Arcola's Studio K), *Everything Must Go!* and *This Wide Night* (Soho Theatre),

The Mother Ship, How to Tell the Monsters from the Misfits (Birmingham Rep), *The Country* (Salisbury Playhouse), *Desire Lines, The Snow Queen* (Sherman, Cardiff), *Small Miracle* (Tricycle/ Mercury, Colchester- Best Design TMA awards), *The Wild Party* (Rosie Kay Dance Company) and The Shy Gas Man (Southwark Playhouse).

Designs for opera include: *The Magic Flute* (English Touring Opera), *War and Peace* (Scottish Opera/ Royal Scottish Academy of Music and Drama), *The Cunning Little Vixen, Orpheus in the Underworld* (Royal College of Music) and *La Calisto* (Early Opera Company).

Mike Beer   Sound Designer

Mike started his career at the Sherman Theatre Cardiff 1986. Since then he has toured Theatre and Corporate events worldwide over the last 20 years with Companies including DV8 Physical Theatre, Theatre Royal Bath, Bristol Old Vic, Diversions Dance, West Yorkshire Playhouse, Birmingham Stage, Theatr Clwyd, Act Productions, Fiery Angel, Theatre Gwynedd, Imagination, Sony, and Ford Motor Car Company. Mike's designs include: *Coasting* and *Treasure Island* (Bristol old Vic), *A Provincial Life, The Passion, Love Steals Us From Loneliness* and *The Persians* (National Theatre Wales), *Deffro'r Gwanwyn* (Theatr Genedlaethol Cymru), *BFG* (Fiery Angel), *Great Expectations* (Aberystwyth Art Centre), *Desire Lines, The Borrowers* and *Merlin* (The Sherman Theatre Company), *The Firework Maker's Daughter* and *Danny the Champion of the World* (Birmingham Stage Company), *Single Spies, Legal Fictions* and *The Importance of Being Earnest* (The Theatre Royal Bath), Don *Quixote* (West Yorkshire Playhouse).

Much of Mike's work for the last 5 years has been with Stage Sound Services, working as Sound designer and production consultant on Theatre and Corporate events.

Natasha Chivers   Lighting Designers

Theatre/Opera credits include: *A Few Man Fridays* (Cardboard Citizens), *Alice in Wonderland* (Royal & Derngate), *Judgement Day* (Print Room), *27* and *The Wheel* (National Theatre of Scotland), No Sweat (Generating Company), *One Monkey Don't Stop The Show* (Eclipse Theatre), *Happy Days* (Sheffield Crucible), *Chekhov in Hell* (Plymouth Theatre Royal), *And The Horse You Rode In On* (Told By An Idiot), *Zaide* (Classical Opera/Sadlers Wells), *The House of Bernarda Alba, Empty/Miracle Men, Home* and *Mary Stuart* (National Theatre of Scotland), Statement of Regret (National Theatre), *Sunday in the Park With George* (Wyndhams Theatre), *The Wolves in the Walls* (NTS/Improbable), *That Face* (Royal Court Theatre/West End), *Playhouse Creatures* and *Jerusalem* (West Yorkshire Playhouse), *Othello, Dirty Wonderland, Pool* (No Water), *Peepshow, Hymns and Sell-Out* (Frantic Assembly).

Dance credits include: *Electric Hotel* (Sadlers Wells/Fuel), *God's Garden* (Arthur Pita/Open Heart/Linbury), *Electric Counterpoint* (Royal Opera House) and *Scattered* (Motionhouse-Tour/QEH). *Natasha won a Theatre Award* UK in 2011 for *Happy Days* (Best Design) and an Olivier Award in 2007 for *Sunday in The Park With George* (Best Lighting Design).

Why I'm Writing a Play about Bradley Manning

Tim Price

This article was first published by the Guardian Online
on 16 December 2011

www.guardian.co.uk/stage/theatreblog/2011/dec/16/
bradley-manning-wikileakstheatre-wales

I'm haunted by Manning's journey from Pembrokeshire schoolboy to US soldier facing life imprisonment for leaking state secrets.

Today, one day before his 24th birthday, Bradley Manning will start the process that will determine whether he'll celebrate his next 30 birthdays behind bars. I will be watching every minute of this case, because for the past year I have been writing a play entitled *The Radicalisation of Bradley Manning* for National Theatre Wales.

I have been following Bradley's case since his arrest in May 2010. His story had a heady mix of espionage, geo-politics and cyber-frontierism, but it wasn't until I learned of Bradley's teenage years in Wales that my curiosity turned into obsession.

This young soldier – who has attempted to call the president of the US as a defence witness – knows bus timetables around Haverfordwest. He knows the trials of schoolboy rugby, and speaks rudimentary Welsh. Once I realised this, Bradley became more than a news story. We had things in common. So reading accounts of his torture in the Quantico brig haunted me.

While his treatment shocked me, his alleged actions thrilled me. If Bradley is guilty of uploading the information to WikiLeaks then he has courageously reminded us that not only is finance, religion, media, manufacturing and politics transnational, but so is our morality. At a meeting with National Theatre Wales to discuss the production of another of my plays, I could not get the young soldier out of my head, and confessed to the theatre that I believed we were doing the wrong play. I had to write about Manning, I told them, and they had to produce it. (It wasn't as finger-snappy as that, of course – I did shoe-gaze and apologise a lot.)

National Theatre Wales agreed, and to my eternal gratitude we switched plays. At a meeting with super-swish lawyers Harbottle & Lewis (of phone-hacking fame) we were told that several of our legal worries were 'novel'. Novel in the sense that there was neither case law nor legal precedent for many of the questions we were asking. Could we use some of the leaked material on stage? Was there a public-interest defence for work shown in a theatre? Could we libel real people in Bradley's life? Could the US military sue?

I've only written two plays, so I still feel inexperienced. I constantly ask myself if I'm the right person for the job. But I have made a commitment to myself, National Theatre Wales and to Bradley Manning to tell his story with as much integrity as I can summon.

On 16 December Manning goes to court, where the US military will paint him as a villain. He will return to his cell, where he will receive delivery of more birthday cards than he's probably had on all his birthdays put together. Among the cards from every country touched by the WikiLeaks scandal, there will be one from me. I urge you to take the time to get in touch with this young man who is accused of changing the world.

Thanks

John McGrath, Lucy Davies and all at National Theatre Wales,
Nicky Lund, Matthew Aubrey, Gwawr Loader, Kyle Rees, Harry Ferrier,
Anjana Vasan, Sion Daniel Young, Remy Beasley, Ryan Hacker,
Alex Beckett, Bethan Witcomb, Sam Jones, Meredydd Barker,
Orla O'loughlin, James Doyle-Roberts, Richard Lakos, Naomi Colvin,
Anthony Timmons, Ben Griffin, Ciaron O'Reilley, Lindi Carter,
Genny Bove, Vicky Moller, Tom Dyer, Kim Zetter, Melanie Corp,
Ann Clwyd MP, Guy Grandjean, Alex Needham, Gary Marsh,
Mark Jefferies, John Llewelyn Jones, Chloë Moss, Philip Price,
Menna Price, Matthew Price, Maryline Price, Sophia Price

The Radicalisation of
Bradley Manning

For my parents

The story I tell happened in a time
we cannot understand.

Jorge Luis Borges

I will officially give up on the society we have
if nothing happens.

Bradass87

Courage is contagious.

Billy Graham

Characters

in order of appearance

Bradley Manning, *fourteen to twenty-three, US soldier, accused of leaking the largest amount of classified material in history – to be played by every member of cast*

Marine 1, *guard in Quantico brig*

Chorus, *see author's note*

Mrs Stokes, *fifties, inspirational history teacher*

Class, *Tasker Milward V C School*

Mark Pritchard, *fourteen to seventeen, Welsh teenager, class charmer*

Gavin Hope, *fourteen to seventeen, Welsh teenager, class thug*

Lisa Williams, *fourteen to seventeen, Welsh teenager, class beauty queen*

Anthony Edwards, *fourteen to seventeen, Welsh teenager, class whipping boy*

Marie, *Bradley's colleague at Zoto*

Al, *thirties, director of photo-sharing website Zoto*

Customer, *any age*

Tina, *Bradley's colleague in the US service industry*

Brian Manning, *fifties, Bradley's father*

Waitress, *any age*

Drill Sergeant, *instructor for United States Army Basic Training*

Recruit 1, *fellow recruit of Bradley's to the US military*

Recruit 2, *fellow recruit of Bradley's to the US military*

Recruit 3, *fellow recruit of Bradley's to the US military*

Reporter, *news reporter for Syracuse.com at Proposition 8 rally*

Tyler Watkins, *twenty, gay student, Bradley's first love*

Marine 2, *marine at Quantico brig*

Marine 3, *marine at Quantico brig*

Marine 4, *marine at Quantico brig*

Kyle, *twenty, hacker*

Alison, *twenty, hacktivist*

Shazia, *hacker*

Commander Browning, *marine in charge of Quantico brig*

Soldier 1, *soldier stationed at the Discharge Unit, awaiting dismissal from the army*

Soldier 2, *soldier stationed at the Discharge Unit, awaiting dismissal from the army*

Soldier 3, *soldier stationed at the Discharge Unit, awaiting release from the army*

Sergeant Miles, *Bradley's 'battle buddy', assigned to Bradley at the Discharge Unit to help with the stress of transition from army to civilian life*

Major, *stationed at the Discharge Unit, tasked with recycling Bradley back into the army*

Intel Officer 1, *fellow intelligence analyst of Bradley's at Forward Operating Base Hammer*

Intel Officer 2, *fellow intelligence analyst of Bradley's at Forward Operating Base Hammer*

Iraqi Federal Police (IFP)

Nidal, *Iraqi Federal Police*

Major, *translator in charge of Bradley's Division*

Deaf Counsellor, *US military counsellor*

Blind Counsellor, *US military counsellor*

Mute Counsellor, *US military counsellor*

Commander, *US military commander in charge of Forward Operation Base Hammer in Iraq*

Author's Note

Throughout the play there are stage directions for the Chorus. These are just suggestions. All direction for the Chorus should be discovered by the director and cast in rehearsal. The Chorus should be on stage at all times, and should serve the story by creating the subtext of the scene – through physical language as well as by bringing fluidity to the transitions between time and space. The cast should seek to blur the lines between characters and choral personalities, so that the Chorus serves as a five-headed monster, holding the play together by pulling it apart.

Every actor must play Bradley at some point. Throughout the play there are stage directions suggesting when to use this device, but it is at the director's discretion, provided every company member plays Bradley. Lines in bold were spoken chorally in the first production, but this is also at the director's discretion.

/ indicates when the next line should be spoken.

// indicates the next following line should also interrupt.

– indicates an interruption by another thought or character.

Scene One

March 2011.

Bradley *on 'Prevention of Injury' watch in Quantico brig.*

Darkness.

Bradley *lies in a smock on a bench.*

Marine 1 (*offstage*)   Detainee 4333453, are you okay?

Beat.

Bradley   What?

Marine 1 (*offstage*)   Answer affirmative or negative. Are you okay?

Beat.

Clanking sound of door opening . . .

Scene Two

Present day.

Chorus 1   Bradley Manning is a traitor.

Chorus 2   Bradley Manning is a hero.

Chorus 3   Bradley Manning is a f***ing a-hole.

Chorus 4   Bradley Manning is a soldier.

Now **Chorus** *speaks at the same time, over each other, getting louder and louder trying to be heard.*

Chorus 5   Bradley Manning is a sign of the times.

Chorus 6   Bardley Manning should fry!

Chorus 1   Bradley Manning is going to die in jail.

Chorus 2   Bradley Manning is not going to get a fair trial.

Chorus 3   Bradley Manning is a human rights issue.

Chorus 4   Bradley Manning is being held in inhumane conditions.

Chorus 5   Bradley Manning is an intelligence analyst.

Chorus 6   Bradley Manning should not have enlisted.

Chorus 1   Bradley Manning needs our help.

Chorus 2   Bradley Manning is only a boy.

Chorus 3   Bradley Manning caused the Arab Spring.

Chorus 4   Bradley Manning is gay!

Chorus 5   Bradley Manning was tortured.

Chorus 6   Bradley Manning was held in Kuwait.

Chorus 1   Bradley Manning's glasses were taken from him, which is a contravention of his human rights.

Chorus 2   Bradley Manning is a whistleblower.

Chorus 3   Bradley Manning is innocent.

Chorus 4   Bradley Manning is not a machine.

Chorus 5   Bradley Manning is a hotheaded loner.

Chorus 6   Bradley Manning is twenty-three.

Chorus 1   Bradley Manning is meh . . .

Chorus 2   Bradley Manning is in chains twenty-three hours a day.

Chorus 3   Bradley Manning is a communist.

Chorus 4   Bradley Manning should never have gone to Iraq, whose idea was that?

Chorus 5   Bradley Manning took an oath to serve his nation, and abide by the rules and regulations of the armed forces.

Chorus 6   Bradley Manning is a complex character deserving of our compassion.

Chorus 1   Bradley Manning was tired of being a victim.

Chorus 2   Bradley Manning's personal and sexual issues inform his decisions.

Chorus 3   Bradley Manning was let down by those above him, and if this is anyone's fault it's the army. And don't ask don't tell.

Chorus 4   Bradley Manning was a witness to war crimes.

Chorus 5   Bradley Manning went too far.

Chorus 6   Bradley Manning is the WikiLeaks guy, right?

Chorus 1   Bradley Manning was recycled.

Chorus 2   Bradley Manning is our Dan Ellsberg.

Chorus 3   Bradley Manning has security clearance.

Chorus 4   Bradley Manning was the kid who got all aggro on *The X Factor*, right? Right?

Chorus 5   Bradley Manning sounds like a real cool guy, at least before they sent him crazy in detention.

Chorus 6   Bradley Manning knew when he leaked all of those records he had a pretty good idea he was going to pay for it down the road. He still did it. That's not cowardly.

Chorus 1   Bradley Manning is a fucking hero no matter how a trial plays out.

Chorus 2   Bradley Manning is just a dumb kid, and his actions really haven't changed anything.

Chorus 3   Bradley Manning worked at Starbucks.

Chorus 4   Bradley Manning didn't know what was in the cables he leaked.

Chorus 5   Bradley Manning's commentators have presumed he's guilty.

Chorus 6   Bradley Manning is guilty of nothing at this time.

Chorus 1   Bradley Manning saw what looked like a pattern of wrongdoing.

Chorus 2   Bradley Manning's case serves to illustrate how badly designed US military networks are in terms of supporting information compartmentalisation and secrecy silos.

Chorus 3   Bradley Manning is a dickhead of colossal dimensions.

Chorus 4   Bradley Manning is rotting in the brig.

Chorus 5   Bradley Manning is too trusting.

Chorus 6   Bradley Manning is alleged to have released extensive US military and government materials to WikiLeaks. These show how the US and many other governments so often say one thing in public, another in private, and yet a third through their actions.

Chorus 1   Bradley Manning needs a bullet in the fucking head.

Chorus 2   Bradley Manning is no hero and neither is Julian Assange.

Chorus 3   Bradley Manning's actions are down to his frustrated sexuality and personal isolation.

Chorus 4   Bradley Manning is why we don't have gays in the military.

Chorus 5   Bradley Manning is still a soldier.

Chorus 6   Bradley Manning hadn't read hardly any of the stuff he leaked.

Chorus 1   Bradley Manning is a transvestite.

Chorus 2   Bradley Manning discovered his company was run by the mob.

Chorus 3   Bradley Manning is now left with the sinking feeling he doesn't have anything left.

Chorus 4   Bradley Manning is not allowed to hold a gun any more.

Chorus 5   Bradley Manning is woken every twenty minutes.

Chorus 6   Bradley Manning's prison guards are being targeted by Anonymous.

Chorus 1   Bradley Manning likes Pi Day.

Chorus 2   Bradley Manning leaked footage of another botched job by your shitty and unprofessional military.

Chorus 3   Bradley Manning is a little squirt who betrayed his country and has risked the lives of all of us. This has been a lesson in what happens when you let homos in the army.

Chorus 4   Bradley Manning wants to work in the prison library.

Chorus 5   Bradley Manning is bipolar.

Chorus 6   Bradley Manning heads our reader poll for who should win this year's Nobel Peace Prize.

Chorus 1   Bradley Manning worked at Abercrombie & Fitch.

Chorus 2   Bradley Manning is not a piece of equipment.

Chorus 3   Bradley Manning has an iPhone.

Chorus *moves into position so that* **Mrs Stokes** *stands in front of a classroom of kids.*

Chorus 4   Bradley Manning is moving to a less harsh detention centre.

Chorus 5   Bradley Manning wants an air purifier.

Mrs Stokes   Bradley Manning is Welsh!

Scene Three

October 2001.

Tasker Milward V C School.

Mrs Stokes   So I don't want to hear any bullying or joking about his accent. He can play for Wales, so he has as much right to be here as any of you. Bradley?

The entire room looks at **Bradley** *who stands in the corner of the room holding a piece of paper – his timetable. Ad lib* **Class** *muttering and talking.*

Bradley   Um . . . I don't know if I'm in the right period.

Class *sniggers at his accent and 'period' – some imitate.*

Mrs Stokes   Bradley, within this room you will find people you will love and people you will hate, I know I do. Mr Pritchard, / I assign Mr Manning, // it is your duty to get him to his next class and to make sure no one sticks his head down the toilet until at least Thursday.

Mark   No no no no! Not me.

Gavin   Bummers!

Mrs Stokes   Bradley what do you know about the Norman invasion of Wales?

Bradley   Who's Norman?

Class *erupts into hilarity.*

Lighting state change.

Class *continues to laugh in silence as* **Mark** *walks* **Bradley** *around the room – an opportunity for* **Mark** *to pick out audience members as fellow pupils.*

Mark   Okay! Quickest way to Tesco's is through the lady's garden. Stick with us TASK boys, avoid the ERM lot. Back here's the wasters. Don't lend him anything. She cries when she has her period. His dad got caught with a rent boy. England supporter.

Beat.

Hard (**Gavin**). Wanker (**Anthony**). Psycho (**Lisa**). Stokesy's alright, for a teacher. Keep hold of your bag and don't take a shit in school.

Sequence over: **Class** *noise returns, normal lighting.*

Mrs Stokes   Settle down! Bradley, you'll get up to speed in no time. Having defeated King Harold in 1066, why did William the Conqueror build Chepstow Castle in 1067, Mr Pritchard?

Mark   He wanted a palace.

Mrs Stokes   Mr Hope?

Gavin *shrugs.* **Class/Chorus** *is permanently harassing, giggling and talking to each other to grotesque degrees, isolating* **Bradley**.

Mrs Stokes   Anyone? Ms Williams?

Lisa   Was it? Was it because . . . right, was it because he wanted to get away from where they'd just had a fight? Where was it?

Anthony   Has / tings.

Lisa   Hastings! I thought it was somewhere else then for a second. So, because he'd won there, did he want to like get far away from there so, they couldn't come back at him. I don't know where's Hastings?

Mrs Stokes   Mr Manning? Hazard a guess?

Silence.

Bradley   I, don't know.

Mrs Stokes   Why does it look like we're going to invade Afghanistan?

Bradley   The Taliban are / hiding bin Laden.

Gavin   Ye-haw!

Mrs Stokes   Thank you, Mr Hope. Throughout history the invaded countries have changed, but the reasons stay the same. *Strategy* drives America to invade Afghanistan, and *strategy* . . . drove William the Conqueror to build a fort at the edge of Wales.

A piece of paper hits the back of **Bradley***'s head.*

Mrs Stokes   Through / military might and intermarriage / / the Normans went on to take control of Wales.

Bradley (*under*)   What was that for?

Mark (*under*)   Don't.

More paper flies at **Bradley**. **Lisa** *and* **Anthony** *throw pieces of paper at* **Bradley**.

Bradley   What the fuck?

The frenzy of throwing stops as **Mrs Stokes** *turns.*

Mrs Stokes   What's going on? Bradley?

Silence.

She turns her back again.

'The Mailed Fist', as it was known, gripped Wales following the Norman Conquest.

More paper flies, **Anthony** *throws some paper and it hits* **Mark**, *who takes umbrage at* **Anthony** *joining in.* **Mark** *stands up to throw paper at* **Anthony**, *but* **Mark** *becomes the target and gets totally plastered by the rest of the* **Class**.

Mark *is overwhelmed until* **Bradley** *joins in, steps in front of* **Mark** *and defends him, hurling paper back at* **Anthony**.

Mrs Stokes *turns around and the* **Class** *immediately reverts to good behaviour. But* **Bradley** *is too slow. He is left standing alone pelting paper at* **Anthony**.

He realises he's alone.

Mrs Stokes   Bradley Manning. See me after class.

Bradley   It wasn't just me.

Mrs Stokes   You are the only one I saw.

Bradley   I'm not lying.

Mrs Stokes   You were the only one I saw.

Bradley   But that's / bullshit. I'm not lying.

Mrs Stokes   I won't ask you again.

Bradley   But –

Mrs Stokes   I won't tell you again.

Bradley   WHY WON'T YOU LISTEN?

Scene Four

August 2010.

Quantico brig.

Marine 1   Contravenes regulations.

Beat.

No exercise.

Bradley   I'm / just –

Marine 1   No exercise.

Bradley   I am still a soldier.

Marine 1   No exercise.

Bradley   What's the problem?

Scene Five

December 2005.

Bradley *at Zoto.*

Chorus *comforts* **Marie** *and pulls* **Al** *away from* **Bradley.**

Al   Nothing, I just need a word with you.

Bradley   Okay.

Al   How's things?

Bradley   Great. I wanted to talk to you actually, you're going to love this, I've just created a platform, it's at alpha stage so you can take a look at it, for video sharing in Flash.

Al   That's great, Brad.

Bradley   I think our users are ready for this kind of diversification, I've got a couple of independent tools / working, I just need to spend some time integrating them into an OS.

Al   Brad. Brad. Okay, Brad. Listen. Bradley!

Beat.

You've done some great work. Corey's been telling everyone. Your stuff with Ajax.

Beat.

Got no complaint with your work.

Beat.

You shout at Marie?

Bradley   I didn't shout at Marie.

Beat.

We had an argument.

Al   Lose your temper with her?

Beat.

Raise your voice with her? You did raise your voice to her didn't you?

Beat.

Bradley   Yes. But she raised her voice at me, and it's just because she doesn't understand stuff that I have to explain things to her like a hundred times, about ssql or whatever, and try to keep on top of my own work.

Al   Marie's upset, Bradley.

Beat.

You okay with Marie being upset?

Bradley   Are you okay with her not being able to do her job?

Al   I don't think the problem's with Marie.

Beat.

Part of the job, Bradley, is to be a co-operative. Part of the job is not to take up my time sorting out conflict.

Bradley   There's no conflict, she just needs to learn how to do her job.

Al   Job isn't just managing content. It's being courteous. Co-workers.

Bradley   I am courteous.

Al   Why don't you answer people?

Beat.

Bradley   I don't know. / I don't hear them.

Al   Kind of rude, don't you think?

Bradley   I guess.

Al   If I've had one complaint about you refusing to answer people, I've had a hundred.

Silence.

Al   I liked the idea of having an upstart kid around. Keep us on our toes. But you just ain't professional, Bradley. Sort of need everyone on the team.

Bradley   I am / on the team.

Al   Marie wouldn't agree. See where I'm coming from?

Bradley   I'm trying to do my job.

Al   Y'do great work, Bradley.

Beat.

Quite often I look at you, and you're staring into space.

Bradley   I'm the best developer / you've got.

Al   Don't have time to be dealing with this.

Bradley   If Marie would just listen, she wouldn't need to ask me the same things over and over every time we have a crash.

Al   Marie will learn. I don't think you will.

Bradley   I promise I won't shout at her again.

Al   Sorry, Bradley. Gotta let you go.

Silence.

Bradley   I'll listen more.

Al   I believe you believe that. But you're too young for us. Made a mistake hiring you.

Bradley   I'll listen more.

Beat.

I'm the best developer you've got.

Al   You make Marie cry.

Beat.

She's a friend.

Beat.

Been here since the start.

Silence as **Bradley** *digests this.*

Bradley   There's no way I can, go on like a, like a probation thing? I can prove to you –

Silence.

Oh God.

Beat.

My old man. He's gonna flip He's . . . Oh God.

Beat.

You still like me, right?

Scene Six

October 2001.

Tasker Milward V C School.

Mrs Stokes   I like all my pupils, Bradley, it's just you seem to have a problem with authority. Do you have a problem with authority?

Beat.

Why were you arguing with me?

Bradley   Because it's not fair.

Mrs Stokes   Who are you to say what's fair and what's not?

Bradley   Who are you to?

Pause.

Mrs Stokes   Think you've just answered my first question there, Bradley.

Beat.

Listen. This is a new school. New teachers. New classmates.

Beat.

You're already at a huge disadvantage. You're American;
you've joined late; you're not a big lad. You don't need to add
a bad attitude to that mix.

Beat.

How's things at home?

He shrugs.

Mrs Stokes   Okay, next time you feel yourself filling up
with anger, I want you to take a deep breath. Once you've
taken that deep breath all your anger will go away and you'll
have clarity. You'll know what you should do next, and I
guarantee it will never be lash out.

Beat.

Will you try that for me?

He nods.

Mrs Stokes   Who threw the first paper ball?

Bradley   Gavin, miss. Is that everything?

Scene Seven

April 2006.

Bradley *in a McJob, Tulsa, Oklahoma.*

Customer   Yes, just the soya latte.

Bradley   Flat white soya latte?

Tina *hands the cup to* **Bradley** *who hands it over to the* **Customer**.
Chorus *performs service industry jobs, and ensures* **Bradley** *and*
Tina *have the right props.*

Customer   Thank you.

Bradley   Sorry for the . . .

Customer *has left.*

Bradley *yawns.*

Tina   So where you living now?

Bradley   I was at my dad and stepmom's for a while, didn't really belong there, so I got my own place in Midtown. Landlord's kind of a crappy.

Tina   Okay.

Bradley   I'm just doing this till I get my own tech company up and running. Last place was a fucking joke. I'm not here long so, it's okay.

They start folding shirts.

Tina   Everyone's just here for the summer.

Bradley   Yuh.

Tina   What's that supposed to mean?

Silence.

You think I want / to work here for ever?

Bradley   No.

Beat.

I didn't mean that.

Beat.

I don't know what I meant.

Silence.

They stand at a counter with a factory line of burgers on it. They assemble a burger together.

Beat.

Bradley   I'm not being mean.

Tina   You are.

Bradley   Forget it.

Silence.

Tina   My friend lives in Midtown, whereabouts?

Bradley   Uh, Brady Arts District, around there.

Beat.

I'm just saying. I've lived in the UK. I've built websites. I practically nursed my mom on my own. I'm sorry if that's made me want to do something with my life.

She squirts the surface with a cleaning product, he mops the floor.

Bradley   These people don't. So I have nothing in common with them.

Beat.

If that makes me mean. Then fine. I'm mean.

Tina   You haven't tried talking to everyone.

Bradley   I have.

Tina   Really?

Bradley   Yes. Most of them.

Tina   Most of them.

Bradley   They don't wanna do anything with their lives. I can tell. There's no rush. I can't get out of here quick enough.

Tina   You look down on / people, Bradley.

Pause.

Bradley   Maybe I do. They deserve to be looked down on, if they think this is all they're good for.

They put headsets on.

Tina   Jason said he saw you sleeping in your car.

Beat.

Bradley   I was doing a double shift.

Tina   He's seen you a few times. (*To headset.*) I'm just putting you through to our policy support team, sir. Please hold! (*To* **Bradley**.) You sleep in your car.

Beat.

Bradley   I don't, sleep in my car.

Tina   You're always the last to leave and you have a toothbrush in your drawer.

Beat.

Bradley   I'm a hard worker.

Tina   Everyone's seen you brushing your teeth in the toilet.

Beat.

Bradley   That doesn't mean anything.

Tina   You look down on everyone and walk around telling everyone we're all stupid but you're the one who's homeless.

Beat.

Bradley   I share a place in Midtown.

Tina   I thought it was your *own* place? (*To headset.*) Yes, sir, we're just waiting for one of my colleagues who's on another line. Sorry for the delay.

Beat.

I don't care if you sleep in a dumpster. Just don't act like you're smarter than everyone else. It'll bite you on the ass. You sleep in your car, and work a crappy job. You can't look down on *anyone.* You're just as trapped as the rest of us.

Scene Eight

September 2010.

Quantico brig.

A clunking sound.

A plate of food is slid under the door.

Bradley *approaches it. He looks at* **Tina**.

He picks up his food, sits next to **Tina** *and eats in silence.*

Scene Nine

August 2007.

An American diner.

Another **Bradley** *sits in a diner opposite his father,* **Brian**. **Brian** *is played by the whole chorus.*

Bradley *fiddles nervously with a napkin.*

Bradley   Thanks for meeting me.

Brian   You ate yet? I think I'm going for pancakes. You think pancakes?

Bradley   I'm good.

Brian   You eat yet?

Bradley   I haven't got any / money so –

Brian   I can buy you breakfast, Bradley.

Bradley   Pancakes are fine.

Brian (*to waitress*)   Two pancakes, both with maple syrup.

Brian   I ain't eat here before.

Bradley   It's good. It's / good.

Silence.

Brian (*about the napkin*)   Stop that.

Silence, as **Bradley** *puts the napkin down.*

Brian   You not going to ask how your stepmom is doing?

Bradley   How is she?

Brian   Doing just fine.

Beat.

Getting new carpet. House is a mess.

Silence, as **Bradley** *starts fiddling with the napkin again.* **Brian** *takes it off him.* **Bradley** *takes a deep calming breath.*

Bradley   I uh. I asked to see you today, Dad, because uh . . .

Brian   Where you living now?

Beat.

Bradley   I'm staying. I'm with friends. Around.

Chorus *acts as* **Waitress**, *who brings over two pancakes.*

Bradley   Thank you.

Waitress *becomes another* **Brian**.

Bradley   I wanted to ask you. If uh, if you know, if you could help. If you had. If you could help, me pay my way to go to college.

Two Brians   You been looking at schools?

Bradley   MiT, BU.

Silence.

I'll work. I'm working crappy jobs now, but I need to be going someplace else otherwise, all I am is someone who works crappy jobs. And living, you know, / with nowhere.

Brian   Where are you working now?

Bradley   I was at Abercrombie Fitch. Looking for something else. In between.

Brian   You think the world owes you a career. Well, it doesn't. / Your mother took you to Wales and you lost all sense of reality.

Bradley   This is not because Mom took me to Wales when you walked out on us.

Silence.

Three Brians   You watch your mouth.

Silence.

Eat your pancakes.

Beat.

You want to go to college.

Bradley   Yeah, major in computer sciences.

Silence.

Brian   You think that's going to fix everything?

Bradley   Ye / ah.

Brian   Well it's not.

Bradley   Are you going to help me or not?

*A fourth **Brian** counts out some money and puts it on the table.*

Brian   Take that money. Meet me here tomorrow with a résumé, a clean shirt and tie. We head on down to the military recruitment centre together.

Bradley   No, Dad, I'm not joining the army! I want to go to college!

Brian   When you were a boy all you wanted to do was join the army.

Bradley   I want to go to college.

Brian   What's your problem with the military?

Bradley   I don't have a problem with the military, Dad, it's the government / I have a problem with.

Brian   You get three square meals a day. A roof over your head.

Bradley   I don't know why I thought you'd help.

Brian   You can work with computers in intelligence. They've got the best hardware. You get three square meals, roof over your head and a skill base. And here's the thing. After four years' service, they pay for you to go to college.

Bradley   They pay you to go?

Brian   To any school you want. Ivy League. And they pay you a wage. You have to wait but you're getting life experience and money in your pocket.

A fifth **Brian** *joins and physically leans on* **Bradley**.

Brian   Get your degree and get the hell out of there, with a degree and military credentials.

Silence.

Bradley   I could go to MiT?

Brian   You go where you want. For free.

Silence.

Bradley   I'm five-two and I weigh a hundred / and five pounds.

Brian   You ain't going in for infantry. Basic will be tough.

Bradley   I'm gay.

Beat.

Brian   Life's about compromises. D'you wanna to be a man and join the army, or do you want to be gay and work in Starbucks?

Beat.

Brian *offers him the money.*

Bradley *takes it.*

Bradley   Where do I go?

Scene Ten

September 2002.

Tasker Milward V C School.

Mrs Stokes   The front please, Bradley, take the hot-seat. Today! We are learning about the Merthyr Rising of 1831!

Reluctantly, another **Bradley** *goes to the front of the* **Class** *and sits down.*

Mrs Stokes   A popular rising where the workers took control of the town. A time when revolutionary ideas threatened the status quo. The first time the red flag of revolution was raised in the world.

She leans on **Bradley**.

Mrs Stokes   This twenty-three-year-old man was executed for those ideas. Hanged to death outside the entrance to what is now Cardiff market.

Beat.

But he's come back from the grave for one afternoon to help you pass your GCSEs. So class, let's welcome – (*to* **Bradley**) Dic Penderyn. Who has a question for our hot-seated martyr? Lisa?

Lisa   Um . . . well, uh. Oh, um . . . I was gonna say . . . no. I. Whatyoucall? I had it then. No! Hang on. What's your, what's your real name?

Bradley   Richard Lewis.

Gavin   How old are you?

Bradley   Twenty-three.

Mark   Are you gay?

Class *hilarity.*

Offended, **Bradley** *starts to get out of his seat and give up.* **Mrs Stokes** *indicates for him to take a breath.* **Bradley** *sits down and takes a deep calming breath.*

Bradley   No. I'm not.

Mark   Have you ever kissed a boy?

Mrs Stokes   Thank you Mr Pritchard, I think this line of questioning has been exhausted.

Anthony   What was it like being hanged to death?

Bradley *shrugs.*

Mrs Stokes   Mr Penderyn?

Beat.

The **Class** *is silent.*

Mrs Stokes   You have the class's attention, Mr Penderyn.

Bradley   I didn't like, all the people watching and not doing anything. If I'd seen someone innocent getting punished for no reason I'd do something about it. All these people who I thought were my friends. Just let me die.

Silence.

Mrs Stokes   Just to clarify, Mr Penderyn, there was a petition with over eleven thousand signatures urging the government to release you, but yes. That must have awful for you. What were your last words?

Bradley   I don't remember. I was too busy dying.

The **Class** *laughs.* **Bradley** *enjoys the moment.*

Mrs Stokes   Your last words were '*Oh arglywdd, dyma gamwedd*'. What do they mean? Test your Welsh.

Bradley   *Arglywdd* is God, right?

Mrs Stokes   'Oh Lord, what an injustice' or 'Oh Lord, here is iniquity'. Why did you say that?

Bradley   Because I'm innocent. I didn't stab that soldier in the leg. I didn't stab anyone, they got the wrong guy.

Gavin   What's it like being a martyr?

Bradley   I'm not a martyr. / That's the frustrating thing, I'm dead but I can't control what happens to my name.

Gavin   You are butt.

Bradley   A martyr is someone who wants to die. I didn't want to die.

Mrs Stokes   That's not necessarily true.

Bradley   It is.

Mrs Stokes   A martyr is someone who died for a cause, not someone who killed themselves for a cause, there's a difference.

Bradley   Okay, well, I'm not a proper martyr.

Mark   What's someone who's not a proper martyr?

Bradley   I'm not a martyr; I just got caught, and got blamed for something I didn't do. How does that make me a martyr?

Lisa   Because you got punished.

Bradley   Those guys that flew the planes into the World Trade Center, they were martyrs. Suicide bombers in Afghanistan, they're martyrs. A martyr is someone who believes in something so much they'll kill themselves for it. Not someone like me who just got caught.

Mrs Stokes   Anyone agree with Mr Penderyn?

Pause.

Anyone want to disagree with him?

Lisa   It's not. It doesn't matter. What it is, is. Like you haven't got to. Just because you haven't done something, if the army or government or whoever make you pay, then . . . I don't know. I just. I don't know.

Mrs Stokes   Why were you protesting?

Bradley   Uh . . . poor working conditions. Debtors' court. Um.

Mrs Stokes   Anyone else?

Mark   Truck shops.

Lisa   Low wages.

Mrs Stokes   You wanted reform? Yes?

Bradley   Yes.

Mrs Stokes   Mr Penderyn. Hanging you to death was a very severe punishment for maiming a soldier. Do you think the government was threatened by your fighting skills or your ideas?

Pause.

You're not very good at fighting, are you?

Bradley   I don't know.

Mrs Stokes   As a government, you can't punish an idea, so you punish the man.

Beat.

And hope it acts as a deterrent. Is it Bradley's actions that threaten? Or the ideas he subscribes to?

Class   Ideas.

Mrs Stokes   What does that make you?

Bradley   A martyr.

Mrs Stokes   Very good, Bradley. Excellent. Round of applause for Bradley.

Class *claps.*

Scene Eleven

October 2007.

Basic training at Fort Leavenworth.

Clapping becomes the sounds of military drums.

Chorus *and* **Bradley** *become part of a unit, performing fitness training – squat thrusts, burpies, calisthenics. Platoon marches to company area led by* **Drill Sergeant***. They perform the 'bag drill'.*

Drill Sergeant   My name is Sergeant Adams! You may call me 'Sergeant'. You may not call me 'sir'. I work for my money. Why are you blinking like that?

Recruit 1*'s eye twitches.*

Recruit 1   It's a nervous / thing, Sergeant.

Drill Sergeant   Stop blinking.

Beat.

STOP BLINKING.

Beat.

STOP BLINKING.

Beat.

I am your drill sergeant for BCT. The Patriot Phase of your training. Most of you will quit. I want you to quit. I don't want weak soldiers. I don't want soldiers I cannot trust. I don't want soldiers who think for themselves. I want soldiers who think for their platoon. WHY ARE YOU STILL BLINKING? STOP IT!

Beat.

Everyone empty your bags on the ground in one pile.

Recruits *empty their bags in a pile on the floor.*

Drill Sergeant *scoops up the stuff, messes it about, walks all over it, and then gets a gets a stopwatch out.*

Drill Sergeant   Thirty seconds to reclaim your property. Move!

He blows a whistle.

Screen shows a thirty-second countdown clock.

Recruits *scramble for their stuff; immediately it's a nightmare of pushing, shoving, arguing, and* **Bradley** *gets consumed in the mêlée. He vanishes.*

Another **Bradley** *is thrown out of the group – he is isolated and can't get to his property.*

Thirty seconds is up: whistle blows.

None of the **Recruits** *has their stuff.*

Drill Sergeant   Fail! Empty your bags again.

Recruits *reluctantly empty their stuff in a pile again.*

Drill Sergeant *approaches* **Bradley**.

Drill Sergeant   Name!

Bradley   Bradley Manning, Sergeant!

Drill Sergeant   Are you the runt of the platoon, Bradley Manning?

Bradley   I don't think so, Sergeant!

Drill Sergeant   I think you are. Are you going to prove me wrong, Bradley Manning?

Bradley   Yes / Sergeant!

Drill Sergeant   Until then what are you?

Bradley   I don't understand, Sergeant.

Drill Sergeant   I think you're the runt until you prove me wrong. So what are you?

Beat.

WHAT ARE YOU?

Beat.

WHAT ARE YOU?

Recruit 1   Say you're the runt.

Drill Sergeant   Am I talking to you, recruit?

Recruit 1   No, Sergeant.

Drill Sergeant   On the floor. Twenty.

Recruit 1 *starts press-ups.*

Drill Sergeant   What are you, Manning?

Bradley   I'm . . . I'm the, the runt, Sergeant.

Drill Sergeant   What?

Bradley   I'm the runt, Sergeant.

Drill Sergeant   Louder.

Bradley   I am the runt, Sergeant.

Drill Sergeant   I can't hear you.

Bradley   I AM THE RUNT, SERGEANT.

Drill Sergeant *blows his whistle. Thirty-second countdown clock starts.*

Bradley *is slow off the mark, unnerved by the bullying.*

This time it's an even more ruthless scramble for property, **Bradley** *fights tooth and nail to get some stuff. Another* **Bradley** *pops out of the mêlée.*

Drill Sergeant *blows his whistle.*

There is still property on the floor.

Drill Sergeant *empties everyone's bag again, scoops up all the stuff, messes it up, walks all over it.*

Drill Sergeant   Thirty seconds! Starting from now.

He blows whistle. Thirty-second countdown clock.

Bradley *is reluctant to try.*

Drill Sergeant   Manning! Are you defying an order?

Bradley   No, Sergeant!

He tries to gather some of his things.

Whistle blows.

Another **Bradley** *pops out of the scrum.* **Drill Sergeant** *starts emptying bag, platoon is disappointed.* **Drill Sergeant** *scoops up all the stuff, walks over it, throws it on the floor.*

Drill Sergeant   Thirty seconds.

He blows whistle.

Platoon *starts to work together and sort out their property, passing it to each other.* **Bradley** *still struggles to get all of his stuff.*

Another **Bradley** *pops out of the mêlée. Everyone has a bag packed except* **Bradley** *who is on the floor scrambling for some final pieces.*

Whistle blows.

Drill Sergeant   Empty your bags!

Platoon groans.

Recruit 2   For fuck's sake, Manning.

Drill Sergeant *scoops up all the clothes, jumbles them up and walks over them.*

Recruit 3   Manning, get your shit together this time.

Recruit 1   Let's just help him.

Drill Sergeant   Looks like I'm not the only one who thinks you're the runt, Manning! You fail and the whole platoon gives me fifty.

Whistle blows. Countdown clock starts again.

Recruits scramble. **Bradley** *is exasperated.*

Bradley   Why me?

Scene Twelve

September 2008.

A street protest against Proposition 8.

Reporter   Because of the military reference on your sign. You're a soldier right?

Reporter *puts a microphone in front of a surprised* **Bradley**.

Tyler *watches from a distance.*

Bradley   Who are you with?

Reporter   Syracuse.com. What's your name?

Bradley   How about I just don't tell you my name? Best way to keep a secret is to never have it.

Reporter   That's fine.

Bradley   I'm here to protest against Proposition 8. I'm currently serving in the military awaiting deployment to Iraq. I was kicked out of home and once lost my job because I'm gay. The world is not moving fast enough for us as home, work or the battlefield.

Reporter   Is 'Don't Ask Don't Tell' the worst part about being in the military?

Bradley   Totally.

Tyler *catches* **Bradley**'s *eye.*

Bradley   My job, is about life and death, you'd think the army would value personal integrity. Instead they'd rather ten per cent of their employees lie and mislead every single day about who they really are. Excuse me . . .

Bradley *leans towards* **Tyler** *and* **Chorus** *holds him back.*

Bradley   Hey?

Tyler *looks* **Bradley** *up and down.*

Tyler   Hello.

Bradley   I'm Brad.

Tyler   Tyler.

Bradley   Are you going to the rally?

Tyler   Probably, not.

Bradley   Oh.

Tyler   Speeches bore me.

Bradley   Me too, yeah.

They start to walk together.

Tyler   I'm guessing small town, something geeky, web developing, something with good health insurance.

Bradley   Soldier.

Tyler *laughs.*

I am.

Beat.

I'm with the 10th Mountain Division. (*Off* **Tyler**'s *bemusement.*) I'm an intelligence analyst.

Tyler   Computers.

Bradley   Any kind of intelligence, cell, pamphlets.

Tyler   Computers / right?

Bradley   Basically computers, yeah.

They laugh, as they follow the march.

Tyler   You like it?

Bradley   I do a really important job. If I do my job well, brief a brigade commander right, I save lives. I feel a great responsibility.

Tyler   Well, good luck with that.

Bradley   I'm not. I don't see myself, having a military career. I figure I can do a couple of years, get some kick-ass credentials. Get into politics. Pull ideas together.

Tyler   I don't even know what shoes to wear and you've got two careers mapped out.

Bradley   If you had my upbringing you'd work on your exit strategies. How about you?

Tyler   Brandeis. Neuroscience major.

Beat.

I'm also a classical musician and drag queen.

Bradley   That's. That's . . .

Tyler   Shall we go / find a bar?

Bradley   Yes. That's. Absolutely. Yes. I. Yes.

Tyler *walks off and* **Bradley** *follows.*

Scene Thirteen

January 2011.

Quantico brig.

A door slams in **Bradley**'s *face.*

Chorus *becomes a 'Free Bradley Manning' protest.*

Bradley *stands up. He listens hard. The chanting gets a little louder.*

He tries to press his ear as close to a wall as possible. The chanting becomes a little clearer. 'Free Bradley, Free Bradley Manning, Free **Bradley** *Manning.'*

Bradley *is stunned. He stands stock still as he tries to digest what he's hearing.*

He is sure. He's hearing 'Free Bradley Manning'.

A sob escapes him, and he tries to compose himself.

He stands listening, with a huge smile on his face.

He stretches his arms out.

He starts to feel the adrenaline and begins to fidget.

He hops up and down, then tries to stand still.

He hops again and this time runs a little in his room. Punching the air. He jumps on his bed and jumps off it. He runs around the cell.

Marine 1 (*offstage*)   No exercise.

Bradley (*delighted*)   Okay!

Bradley *stands still. He can't help himself – he lets out a howl, punches the air and runs around his cell.*

Clunking sound of a door opening.

Pumped up, four **Marines** *enter.*

Marine 1 *applies handcuffs to* **Bradley**, **Marine 2** *applies leg-restraints.*

Marine 1   Attention!

Bradley *stands at attention.*

The **Marines** *pace around.*

Marine 1   Detainee 4333453, at parade rest!

Bradley *stands with his feet shoulder-width apart.*

Marine 2 *sticks his face in* **Bradley***'s face.*

Bradley *tries to look ahead but can't help look at* **Marine 2***.*

Marine 2   Are you eyeballing me, 4333453?

Bradley   No, Sergeant!

Marine 1   Turn left!

Bradley *turns left.*

Marine 3   Don't turn left!

Bradley *corrects his direction.*

Marine 1   I said turn left!

Bradley   Yes, Corporal!

Marine 4: In the *Marines* we reply 'Aye' not 'Yes'. Do you understand, Private?

Bradley   Yes, Corporal.

Marine 3   YOU MEAN AYE!

Bradley   Aye, Corporal.

Marine 1   Turn right.

Marine 2   Don't turn right!

Bradley   Ye – Aye, Sergeant!

Marine 1   I said turn right!

Bradley   Aye, Corporal!

Marine 1   Stand still so we can remove your restraints.

Beat.

I SAID STAND STILL.

Marine 1 *eyeballs* **Bradley***, who starts to shuffle in retreat.*

Marine 1   I told you to stand still!

Bradley   Yes, Corporal, I am standing still.

Marine 4 *approaches* **Bradley** *menacingly.*

Marine 4   I thought we covered this you say 'Aye', not 'Yes', do you understand?

Bradley   Aye / Corporal.

Marine 1 (*screamed*)   STAND STILL!

Bradley   Yes, Corporal, I am standing still! I mean –

Marine 4   Are we going to have a problem? Do you have a problem with following orders?

Marine 2   Do you have an attitude problem, 4333453?

Marine 4   Sergeant asked you question, 4333453.

Bradley *starts to step backwards in fear.*

The **Marines** *loom towards him.*

Marine 2   SERGEANT ASKED YOU A QUESTION.

But **Bradley** *is too scared. He staggers and sits down.*

Bradley   I . . . I . . . I'm not . . . I'm not trying to do anything. I'm just trying to follow your orders.

Marine 4   DO YOU HAVE A PROBLEM WITH ORDERS?

Bradley   I'm. Please, I'm just / trying to follow orders.

Marine 4   DO YOU HAVE A PROBLEM WITH ORDERS?

Silence.

Bradley (*quietly*)   No, Corporal.

Marine 4 *holds his face in* **Bradley***'s face for an age.*

Bradley *looks at the floor.*

The four **Marines** *stand at the corners of a square.*

Marine 1   Commence your recreation, 4333453.

Very long pause.

Marines *stand stiff and straight, contrasting with* **Bradley**'s *slump.*

Slowly, **Bradley** *stands up.*

Keeping within the square the **Marines** *have formed,* **Bradley** *starts to walk.*

It becomes apparent that **Bradley** *is walking figures of eight.*

Scene Fourteen

September 2009.

Tyler's *student house.*

Bradley *walks into* **Tyler**'s *arms and they kiss in a passionate, drunken embrace.*

Tyler *pulls at* **Bradley**'s *clothes.* **Chorus** *pushes and pulls them apart.*

Tyler   Been too long.

Bradley   I know.

Tyler   Get your shirt off, get your shirt off.

He pulls off **Bradley**'s *shirt.* **Bradley** *is covered in bruises.* **Tyler** *startles.*

Tyler   What the fuck is all that?

Bradley   It's okay.

He tries to re-engage **Tyler**, *who resists.*

Bradley   Don't worry about it.

Tyler *turns* **Bradley** *around to see all his bruising.*

Silence.

Bradley   You don't need to be worried / about this, okay? It's my business.

Tyler   This is / your job. Normal people don't get beat up in an office.

Bradley   I fight back.

Why are you looking at me like that?

Beat.

It's fine.

Tyler   Do you have people you can talk to?

Silence.

Bradley   Pete.

Tyler   What does / Pete have to say about all this?

Bradley   Yeah, he talks to me.

Beat.

If he hears me crying.

He stops putting his shirt on and stares at it.

It won't be for much longer anyway.

Tyler   How come?

Silence.

Overwhelmed, **Bradley** *puts his face in his shirt.*

Tyler   Hey.

For a few moments, **Bradley** *holds his face in his shirt.*

Tyler   Come on.

Bradley *recoils from* **Tyler**.

Silence as **Bradley** *gathers himself.*

Bradley   You go to class today?

Tyler   Uh, yeah.

Beat.

Missed the first one, I slept in.

Bradley   Right.

Silence.

Tyler   You can sue them.

Bradley   You sound like such a fucking idiot. Do you know how you sound sometimes?

Beat.

Like a fucking idiot.

Beat.

I'm outta here.

Bradley *gathers his things.*

Tyler   No.

Bradley   Out of my way.

Tyler   Please stay.

Bradley   GET OUT OF MY WAY.

Silence.

Tyler   I've seen guys like this. You don't have to stand for it.

Bradley   What the fuck do you know about anything?

Beat.

I'm going through this every day, so I can be where you are, and you can't even get out of fucking bed for class.

Beat.

I'm beat up every day, I'm called faggot, and runt and chapter fifteen, people spit on me and – I do it to get where you are and you can't get out of fucking bed?

He rips his shirt open.

You wanna stay in bed with this?

Silence.

I only signed up so they'd pay for me to go to college but I'm such a fuck-up I can't even pass basic training!

Beat.

They're kicking me out.

Beat.

So all this? It's for nothing anyway!

Tyler   Why are they kicking you out?

Bradley   Does it matter?

Scene Fifteen

January 2003.

Tasker Milward V C School.

Anthony   Not, not to me.

He sits at a computer.

I'm just saying.

Beat.

You're meant to have a hall pass to be in here.

Bradley *sits at a computer. The two work in silence.*

Bradley   What game you playing?

Chorus *shields the computer from* **Bradley***'s view..*

Anthony   I'm not playing a game.

Bradley   Jesus, Anthony.

Beat.

I'm just asking.

Silence.

Anthony   I'm writing.

Beat.

A programme.

Bradley   Oh yeah?

*He leans into **Anthony**'s screen. **Anthony** quickly hides it.*

Bradley   What is it, secret?

Anthony   It's not finished.

Bradley   I'm building a website.

Silence.

I could help. I'm pretty good with code.

Anthony   Thanks.

Bradley   Do you want help or not?

Beat.

Anthony?

Beat.

*He goes over to **Anthony**'s screen. Again **Anthony** shields it from him.*

Bradley   Let me see.

Beat.

I'm not going to steal anything – I've got enough of my own ideas.

Beat.

Come on.

Anthony *shakes his head.*

Bradley   Why not?

Silence.

Anthony   It's fine. I don't mind if it's going to take ages.

Exasperated, **Bradley** *returns to his computer. They both sit in silence as they work on their projects.*

Anthony   I don't like . . . going on the yard.

Silence.

Bradley *moves over to* **Anthony***'s screen.* **Anthony** *and* **Chorus** *let* **Bradley** *see.*

Bradley   What are we doing here?

Scene Sixteen

November 2008/2003.

Boston University hackerspace/Tasker Milward V C School.

Tyler   I want you to meet some of my computer geek buddies. David!

A group of BU students sit around, checking out hardware.

David   Oh hey! Tyler.

Tyler   This is Bradley. This is more his kind of thing than mine.

David   Okay! Are you familiar with the open software, open hardware movement? 'Builds' is a space where students can advocate for that movement as well as a space for student-led DIY learning to take place.

Beat.

So! Hang around, check things out, if you've got the know-how, share it. We've got the Open Organisation of Lock Pickers coming along to do a demonstration later, and Free Software Foundation dropping by to talk to us too.

David *moves on.*

Bradley   I want to go home.

Tyler   We're here for *you*, this is *your* thing. You need to meet other geeks and I don't know. / Make some new friends.

Bradley   They're *all* students.

Tyler   You're smarter than all these people put together.

Kyle   Hey?

Tyler   Hey.

Kyle   Kyle.

Tyler   Tyler, Bradley.

Kyle   What happened to your face, man?

Pause.

Tyler   He's a soldier.

Kyle   You're a *soldier*?

Bradley   Intel.

Kyle   Wow! Check out this red robot mouse I built.

He produces a remote control and drives a robot mouse into their personal space.

Bradley, **Tyler** *and* **Kyle** *look at the floor, as* **Kyle** *reverses the mouse, turns it around in circles, sends it back and forth.*

Silence.

Tyler   That's great.

Bradley   Yeah great – work.

Tyler *and* **Bradley** *drift away from* **Kyle**.

Bradley   Can we go home?

Tyler   Seriously?

Bradley   I'm about to lose my job and my one chance of going to college, and you bring me to a place full of people

getting computer science majors and all they're doing is
building fucking *robot mice.*

David *overhears this.*

David   So! Bradley, how about you come meet Alison?

Bradley   Um, I don't know.

Tyler *indicates for him to go.* **David** *brings* **Bradley** *over to*
Alison*'s group.*

Tyler *drifts away from* **Bradley** *and joins another group of people
who are sitting around debating and drinking from red plastic cups.*

Alison   Levy outlines six hacker ethics. 'Access to a
computer and anything else that might teach you how the
world works, should be unlimited.' 'All information should be
free.' 'Mistrust authority – promote decentralisation.' Um,
how many have I said? Oh – 'Hackers should be judged on
their hacking, not on anything like education, race, sexuality.'
This is my favourite: 'You can create beauty on a computer.'

David   Six?

Alison   Fuck, man.

David   'Computers can change your life for the better.'

Kyle*'s mouse darts past the group, followed by* **Kyle** *running after it.
Everyone watches him exit, chasing the red robotic mouse.*

Silence.

Alison   I said the thing about not judging anyone, right?

David   Yeah.

Alison   Where we are now. This is the Mesopotamia of
hacking. MiT, BU sort of.

Everyone laughs.

Hacking, cyber activism / this is where it all started.

David   Is she doing her enlightenment / schtick again?

Alison   Yes, I am!

David   She always / does this.

Alison   I'm sharing information!

Everyone laughs at the in-joke.

Okay. When Gutenberg built the printing press it took thirty years for the first porn publication and a *hundred* years for the first scientific journal. We've had our cyber-porn goldrush. Now it's time for our global enlightenment. The printing presses tore down the self-interest of the church in Europe. Web 2.0 will tear down the self-interest of the corporate state.

Beat.

I'm asking how do we do that?

Bradley   Oh, I'm sorry, I thought you knew.

Alison   No I'm, I'd like to know how we do that.

David   I think it's something do with reverse engineering. Have you seen the lock-pickers over there?

Bradley   Yeah. what's that about?

David   It's symbolic.

Alison   Is that like a metaphor for hacking?

David   Shazia! Tell these guys about locks.

Shazia *hands a lock to* **Bradley**. *She gives him a pin.*

Shazia   Hey? So, you guys ever picked a lock? Okay. So there's a mechanism of control that you have to work backwards from.

David   What do the locks represent though?

Shazia   Okay. So when you pick a lock for the first time, you learn that the only barriers in the world, are psychological. You hold the key to your life, not corporations, parents or university administrators.

Alison   And so, the more people who start to think like that . . .

David   The bigger things we can reverse engineer.

Bradley   Like what?

Alison   Anything I guess?

Bradley *pops his lock open – everyone is pleased.*

Tyler   You want to head off before they start chanting?

Bradley   How could we, reverse engineer a government?

Mrs Stokes *picks up a bin.*

Mrs Stokes   By throwing conventional wisdom into this bin.

She drops a book into a bin.

Come on, books in the bin.

Class *scrambles towards the front of the classroom to throw their history books into the bin.*

Today we're looking at the Rebecca Riots of 1839. All of you find a costume.

This action takes place as **Mrs Stokes** *talks.*

Mrs Stokes *lifts another bin up, the class scramble to it and pull out traditional Welsh clothes and start to dress up as traditional Welsh women.* **Anthony** *gets there first, but gets robbed of everything he gets his hands on, so his outfit is the least complete.*

The **Class** *individually giggle and communicate to each other their delight.*

Mrs Stokes   We're going to help you remember some facts about the riots. And we're going to do it by having a riot of our own.

Confusion as she jumps up on to a table and starts stamping on the table.

Who's with me?

Silence.

I said who's with me?

Gavin   What? We're rioting?

Lisa   In class, like? In class.

Mrs Stokes   Yes!

She bangs on the desk.

I said who's with me!

Class (*ad lib*)   I am! Yeah! Fucking come on! Let's do it!

Mrs Stokes   I'm not taking / any more of this! Are you with me?

Class (*ad lib*)   Yeah! Let's go nuts! Come on! Go on, Stokesy! Let's go down town!

*The **Class** get up on the chairs and desks and push chairs around a bit.*

Mrs Stokes   Gavin! Why are you here today?

Gavin   I don't know / I'm. It's!

Mrs Stokes   Who knows why we've come here, dressed as women, in the cold?

Mark   For a meeting!

Mrs Stokes   What am I standing on?

Gavin   Desk!

Anthony   A toll gate!

Mrs Stokes   A toll gate yes! And what are we going to do?

Bradley   Tear it down!

Mrs Stokes   Why?

Bradley   Because we're sick of having to pay every time we go to market!

Class *cheers.*

Lisa   And we're sick of paying tithes to the church!

Class *cheers.*

Mark   I hate the vicar!

Class *cheers.*

Gavin   Vicar's a prick.

Class *cheers.*

Anthony   Wet harvest.

Class *cheers.*

Gavin (*under*)   You can't riot about the weather, or we'll be out every night.

Bradley   English landlords!

Gavin   Sidebars!

Lisa   Poor rates!

Anthony   Taxes!

Lisa   Why are all the landlords English?

Bradley *gets up on the desk.*

Bradley   We're the ones who know how to farm.

Cheers.

Know how to raise cattle and harvest corn! What the fuck does anyone do except collect money?

Cheers.

What does the church do? Except collect money?

Cheers.

What do the landlords do except collect money?

Cheers.

And what do the fucking turnpikes do for us? Collect money!

Class   COLLECT MONEY!

The **Class** *tips over the final tables and wrecks the 'toll gates'.*

In the background **Anthony** *picks up a chair and throws it.*

Anthony   I'm not a fucking pushover!

Silence.

Everyone stares at a panting **Anthony***.*

Mrs Stokes   Anthony, step out of the room.

Silence.

Step outside.

Gavin   Why are you / such a knob, Anthony?

Lisa   You spoil everything.

Mrs Stokes   Step outside, Anthony.

Anthony   But . . .

He leaves the room, **Bradley** *feels terrible for him.*

Mrs Stokes   Right . . . tell me now. Why did the riots keep happening? What did messing up the classroom feel like?

Mark   It was good. I didn't know I knew all that stuff.

Lisa   I've never . . . you know. What it is, I've never done nothing like that before in a classroom. Not with a whatyoucall there. Teacher.

Mrs Stokes   You felt free of normal school rules? Just as these people felt free of the normal rules of society?

Lisa   Yeah.

Gavin   That was awesome.

Mrs Stokes   What do you think, Bradley?

Bradley   I don't know.

Mrs Stokes   If you feel stupid just take a look round at your classmates.

Bradley *looks at his classmates dressed as women.*

The **Class** *giggles.*

I don't know. I guess, for a moment; I didn't feel like –

Mrs Stokes   What?

Bradley   I didn't feel like the new kid.

Beat.

People were listening.

Mrs Stokes   Can you see why the riots kept happening?

Lisa   It was fun.

Gavin   Can we do it in Maths?

Mrs Stokes   I wouldn't recommend it. Anyone else got any thoughts?

Mark   Sort of. Like if. By showing no respect to the toll gate, we sort of got . . .

Bradley   Self-respect.

Mark   Yeah.

Bradley *takes his bonnet off.*

Mrs Stokes   Why is dressing up as women important?

Lisa   That's fun too.

Mrs Stokes   Absolutely. Gives a sense of occasion. There's something else.

Beat.

What did dressing up give you?

Bradley   Anonymity.

Mrs Stokes   And what does that give you?

Bradley   Freedom.

Mrs Stokes   Yes. If society casts you as powerless, why follow society's rules? Put a hoodie on and move freely. Act without compromise. Right, tidy up the class while I talk to Anthony.

Bradley   Miss, I don't think you should punish Anthony.

Mrs Stokes   Take a deep breath, Bradley.

Scene Seventeen

January 2011.

Quantico brig.

Bradley *takes a deep breath and stands to attention.*

Commander Browning *enters.*

Commander Browning   At ease.

Bradley *stands at parade rest.*

Commander Browning   What happened today at recreation call?

Bradley   I was trying to follow orders, sir, but the Marines seemed intent on causing me distress by giving conflicting orders, sir, and demanding I respond as a Marine even though I am not.

Beat.

I'd like to make a complaint sir, I'd like you to investigate / those Marines.

Commander Browning   I am the commander and no one tells me what to do.

Silence.

There a problem, detainee?

Bradley   I'm making a complaint, sir.

Commander Browning   I am the commander here. That means, for practical purposes, I am God.

Silence.

Bradley   Everyone has a boss who they have to answer to.

Commander Browning   Did I hear that right?

Bradley   You still have to follow brig procedures, sir, whatever. It's not my fault if there's a protest outside.

Commander Browning   Marines!

*The **Marines** enter the cell.*

Commander Browning   Place Detainee 4333453 under Suicide Risk Status and POI.

Bradley   What? No! Why are you doing this? I HAVE DONE NOTHING WRONG.

Commander Browning   Strip Detainee 4333453 of his clothes.

*With no ceremony two **Marines** strip **Bradley** of his clothes.*
***Bradley** starts crying.*

Bradley   Why are you doing this to me! What have I done? Please, no? Please! I'm begging you.

Beat.

Tell me what you want me to do and I'll do it!

Beat.

Just tell me! I don't understand! What have I done?

Commander Browning *leaves followed by the **Marines**.*

Bradley *stands naked in the cell crying.*

Scene Eighteen

November 2003/January 2009.

The Tasker Milward computer room/US Army Discharge Unit.

*Another **Bradley** and **Anthony** sit in the computer room.*

Anthony   It's okay. Let me see.

*He fixes something on **Bradley**'s screen.*

Bradley   Mrs Stokes can be a dick.

Anthony   Everyone thinks she's tidy, but . . .

Beat.

Only if you do exactly what she wants.

*The rest of the **Class** enters.*

Mark   Bradders!

Lisa   Bradley!

Gavin   Here he is!

He jumps up on a desk.

We will fight them on the beaches, we will fight them in Wetherspoon's, we will fight them in Pwll! We will fight them in Llanidloes!

Mark   Come on Bradley / give us another speech.

Bradley   I'm in the middle of something, guys.

Gavin   We / will fight them in our underwear! We fight them in their underwear, we will fight them without underwear!

Class   Speee-eeech! Speee-eeech! Speeee-eeech!

*The gang lift **Bradley** up in the air. **Bradley** is laughing, everyone is laughing and joking and throwing him up in the air like a hero. **Anthony** is isolated.*

Bradley (*laughing*)   No, guys, put me down! Put me down! Come on guys, please.

Suddenly the actions turn less playful and **Bradley** *is in pain.*

He screams.

We are now in Fort Leonard Wood, Missouri – the Discharge Unit. **Bradley** *is held by a group of American* **Soldiers** *who are inflicting pain on him.*

Soldier 1   Say 'I am chapter fifteen'!

Bradley   Fuck you!

Soldier 1   Say 'I'm chapter fifteen'!

Bradley   Let me go!

Soldier 1   Say it!

Bradley   Let me go! Get the fuck off me, you fucking assholes, GETOFFME!!

Soldier 1   Say it, Manning! Fucking say it! You like to suck dick and you're a chapter fifteen!

Bradley   AAA / HHHH FUUUCCCKK YOU!

Soldier 1   SAY IT!

Bradley   GETTTT OFFFF MEEEE!

With a huge effort **Bradley** *kicks himself free. The* **Soldier** *and his gang burst out laughing;* **Bradley** *grabs a chair and holds it over his head.*

Bradley   Stay the / fuck away from me!

Soldier 1   What you gonna do / chapter fifteen? Fuck the chair? Come on, pretty boy, let's see you drop your pants and fuck the chair.

Bradley   STAY THE FUCK AWAY.

Soldier 2   Drop your pants.

Silence.

You're on your own, Manning.

Bradley   Stay the fuck away from me, I'm warning you, I'll fucking, I'll fucking kill you.

Soldier 2   What you gonna do? Cry on me?

Soldiers *laugh at* **Bradley**.

Soldier 2   My nephew's tougher than you – he's eight.

Bradley   I'll fucking kill your nephew.

Soldier 2 *starts towards* **Bradley**. **Soldier 3** *holds him back.*

Soldier 3   You know how hard it is to sleep with you crying all the time?

Beat.

Crying and fucking screaming like a bitch.

Beat.

Like some kind of freak.

Beat.

Crying like a baby.

Beat.

Soldier 1   Got anything to say, chapter fifteen?

Beat.

Soldier 1 *goes for* **Bradley**. **Bradley** *swings a chair.*

Soldier 1 *goes for him again.* **Bradley** *swings a chair.*

Bradley *wets himself.*

Soldier 2 *leans into* **Soldier 1** *and points at* **Bradley***'s trousers.*

Soldier 2   Hell, Manning, you just pissed your pants!

Sergeant Miles *enters.*

Everyone tries to act normally.

Sergeant Miles   What the hell is going on here?

Beat.

Specialist Manning, put that chair down.

Pause.

Specialist Manning!

Bradley   NO / SIR!

Sergeant Miles   Put the chair down!

Bradley   NO! I'm fucking . . .

Sergeant Miles   Specialist Manning, this may be a discharge unit but you are not a civilian yet. Put that chair down, that's an order.

Pause.

Bradley *throws down the chair to guffaws and cat-calling from the other* **Soldiers**.

Sergeant Miles   Pick up the chair, Manning.

Chorus   Yeah, pick up the chair, Manning.

Bradley *catches his breath.*

Sergeant Miles   Specialist Manning, pick up the chair.

Beat.

I SAID PICK UP THE CHAIR.

Bradley   I'M NOT A FUCKING PUSHOVER!

Sergeant Miles *grabs* **Bradley** *and drags him towards the door.*

Bradley   No! No! Get off!

Chorus *whoops with delight and laughs at* **Bradley***'s humiliation.*

Bradley   Let go!

Beat!

Let me go! FUCK YOU! I'LL FUCKING KILL YOU!

Bradley *is dragged kicking and screaming out of the door while the* **Chorus** *cheers and laughs at him.*

Scene Nineteen

December 2003.

Tasker Milward V C School.

Mrs Stokes   Silence!

She looks at her table.

Vandalising school property is serious.

Beat.

I want a name.

Beat.

NOW!

Beat.

Who has done this?

She points to the desk.

If I don't get a name, you will all be punished. If you're happy to protect a vandal then you shall be punished like vandals. Mark? Do you know who has carved this disgusting image on my desk.

Mark   No, miss.

Mrs Stokes   Lisa?

Lisa   Didn't see anyone, miss.

Mrs Stokes   Anthony?

Anthony *shrugs.*

Mrs Stokes   Bradley?

Bradley   Didn't see anything, miss.

Mrs Stokes   Gavin?

Gavin   Didn't see nothing, miss.

Mrs Stokes   Fine. I'll see what Mr Roberts has to say about this. All of you will see me after school for detention and I will be speaking to Mr Roberts about getting *all* of your parents involved in this.

Class *groans.*

Bradley   That's not fair.

Mrs Stokes   You have something to say, Bradley?

Bradley   You haven't got to get my mom involved for something I didn't do.

Mrs Stokes   Give me a name and I won't.

Bradley   It's your fault! / You can't say riot in one lesson and then . . .

Mrs Stokes   Shut up, Bradley.

Bradley   What have I done wrong?

Scene Twenty

September 2009.

US Army Discharge Unit.

Major   At ease, Specialist.

Bradley *stands at parade rest, but is ill-disciplined with his posture –*
he is defeated. He has a black eye. The **Major** *goes through some*
paperwork.

Major   Who's supporting you through your discharge
process here?

Beat.

Who's your battle buddy?

Bradley   They keep changing, sir.

Major   Who's it today?

Bradley   Miles.

Major   Miles!

In comes a much bigger, strapping soldier – **Sergeant Miles**, *who*
salutes.

Major   At ease.

Sergeant Miles *stands at parade rest.* **Bradley** *can barely stand*
straight. **Major** *can't look at* **Bradley**.

Major   Specialist, do you know what the term 'recycled'
means.

Sergeant Miles *double-takes.* **Chorus** *gasps and is in shock.*

Bradley   No, sir.

Major   It's a term we use. Sergeant Miles will be familiar,
where the army halts a discharge process. Do you follow,
Specialist?

Bradley   I / guess.

Sergeant Miles   Permission to speak, sir?

Major   Granted.

Pause.

Sergeant   Sir.

Beat.

Are we?

Beat.

Are you saying, Specialist Manning is, uh, to be. Is to be recycled sir?

Major   Yes, Sergeant.

Beat.

There a problem?

Pause.

Sergeant Miles   No, sir.

Major   So, to be clear, Specialist, we have taken a look at the assessments you failed and decided to give you a second chance.

Beat.

We're at war and the army needs you.

Beat.

You will be attached to the 10th Mountain Division as Intel Specialist. You will be . . .

Chorus *plays* **Sergeant Miles***'s disbelief.*

Major   Sergeant Miles.

Sergeant Miles *tries to straighten himself.*

Sergeant Miles   Sir.

Major   You will be deployed to Eastern Baghdad at Forward . . . at Forward Operating –

Beat.

Base.

He clears his throat.

Operating Base –

Staring at the sheet, **Major** *tries to focus, but is distracted by* **Chorus**. **Bradley** *sways.*

Major   Hammer.

He discards the paperwork and takes a moment.

How'd you feel about . . . about serving your country, Bradley?

Bradley *sways.*

Bradley   I'd be proud, sir.

Beat.

I thought I was getting kicked out.

Sergeant Miles *looks to the heavens.*

Major   Good. (*Clears throat.*) Good man.

Sergeant Miles   Permission to speak, sir.

Major   Granted.

Sergeant Miles   Sir, should I take Specialist Manning to speak with the Judge Advocate Group, sir?

Chorus *thinks this is a great idea and is about to bundle* **Bradley** *away when . . .*

Major   I have their paperwork here, they've signed off for recycling. It's all. It's signed off.

Chorus *checks the paperwork and is in shock.*

Major   Your skills, are highly valuable to us Specialist. / Highly valuable.

Bradley   Yes, sir.

Major   We need every, every Intel Specialist we have to be on top of their game, because your Brigade Commander will be relying on your briefings before sending his men into theatre.

Beat.

I hope you realise what an important job you have, Specialist, and what a privilege it is to serve in the US Army.

Bradley   Yes sir, / I won't let you down, sir.

Major   Before . . . Before deployment, you will be stationed in Fort Drum. Good luck, Manning. You're dismissed.

Bradley *straightens himself and gives a proud salute and starts to march to the door.* **Sergeant Miles** *and the* **Major** *share a look before* **Sergeant Miles** *follows* **Bradley**. **Chorus** *prompts* **Sergeant Miles**.

Sergeant Miles   Sir.

Major   Specialist Manning. Do you have . . . do you have anyone, who can support you through deployment?

Bradley   I have met someone, sir.

Major   You have a *girlfriend*, Manning?

Bradley   Yes sir, I do.

Scene Twenty-One

November 2009.

Forward Operating Base Hammer, Eastern Baghdad.

Tableau sequence.

Computers, paperwork, TV screens are on every wall with live feeds from the war as the US engages the enemy.

Post-It notes are on every computer.

Another **Bradley** *stands watching the screens as his fellow* **Intel Officers** *throw stress toys around, mess about and show each other things on screen that make them laugh.*

They are oblivious to **Bradley**, *and they are oblivious to the horrors of war footage being broadcast on the screens.*

Bradley *is drawn to the screens. He can't escape the screens, as everyone else goes about their work.*

Intel Officer 1 *sees* **Bradley** *reading some paperwork and smiling.*

Intel Officer 1   What you got, Manning?

He ecognises the paperwork.

'Specialist Manning's persistence led to the disruption of "Former Special Groups" in the New Baghdad area. Specialist Manning's tracking of targets led to the identification of previously unknown enemy support zones.'

Bradley   Give that back!

He snatches it back from **Intel Officer 1**.

Intel Officer 1   Manning got his first commendation! Make sure you tell your mom.

Bradley   I will.

Intel Officer 1   While you're at it, ask her why you can't grow hair on your balls.

Intel Officers *burst out laughing.*

Waves of digital information code and intelligence crash over **Bradley**, *gradually punishing and exhausting him until he can hardly stand.*

All the time his colleagues do not look at the footage.

Tableau sequence over.

Intel Officer 2   Oh, you seen this new ordinance report?

Bradley   No.

Intel Officer 2   This fucking guy takes a Hellfire right to the head, watch this.

He clicks a video on his screen.

Bradley *watches it.*

Intel Officer 2   Boom! Insane, right?

Beat.

Bradley   Yeah.

Bradley *digests what has happened to him. He leans forward and turns his computer on.*

Intel Officer 2   Boom!

Scene Twenty-Two

April 2004.

Tasker Milward V C School.

Class *erupts –* **Mrs Stokes** *is absent.*

Mark *picks up* **Anthony**'s *bag.*

Anthony   Fuck off, Mark.

Mark   You fuck off.

Mark   Your bag smells of ham. Does anyone need a protractor?

Anthony   Why don't you / fucking pick on someone else Mark? Stop being such a prick to me all the time.

Mark   Is there anything anyone needs? Lisa? Protractor, roller-ruler? This pen's got a compass in it, look at that? That's cool, I'm having that. Bradders, you haven't got a protractor have you?

Anthony   Bradley?

Bradley   Give his stuff back.

Mark   Why? It's Anthony.

Bradley   Mark, come on.

Mark   No way, he's a wanker.

He continues to look in the bag and disregard **Anthony**'s *feelings.*

Unable to take it any more, **Bradley** *grabs the bag from* **Mark** *and hands it to* **Anthony**. **Mark** *retaliates by grabbing it from* **Anthony**. **Bradley** *grabs it from* **Mark**, *there's a tussle and* **Bradley** *finally gets the bag.*

Mark *chases* **Bradley** *around the room while the* **Class** *jeers. The chase ends with* **Bradley** *standing on* **Mrs Stokes**'s *desk.*

The **Class** *falls silent as* **Mrs Stokes** *enters.*

Mrs Stokes   What the hell is going on here?

Mark   He stole my bag, miss.

Mrs Stokes   Get down.

Beat.

NOW!

Bradley *gets down from the table.*

Mrs Stokes   I leave the room for two minutes.

Bradley   Miss.

Mrs Stokes   I don't want your excuses, Bradley. Who wants to go and get Mr Roberts?

Whole **Class** *put their hands up except* **Bradley**.

Scene Twenty-Three

February 2010.

Iraqi Police jail/Forward Operating Base Hammer.

Chorus *are detainees and* **Iraqi Federal Police** (**IFP**).

IFP (*in Arabic*)   KEEP YOUR FUCKING HANDS UP!

The **IFP** *hold guns to the detainees, who have their hands up.*

Bradley   Specialist Manning, / sent from Forward Operating Base Hammer, Major Browning asked me, sent me to assess your detainees.

Nidal   These are insurgents. They distribute Al Qaeda literature.

Beat.

They are insurgents.

One of the **IFP** *beats one of the detainees.*

Bradley   Where were they detained?

Nidal   Out. In street.

Bradley   Okay. They were handing out / insurgency literature, in the street.

Nidal   In the street, yes.

Another of the **IFP** *beats another detainee.*

Bradley   Do you have any of their papers?

Nidal   Nothing.

Bradley   What does this say?

Nidal   'America Must Die'.

Another of the **IFP** *beats another detainee.* **Bradley** *is unnerved.*

Bradley   We need to find out who these people are, what group they're associated with, why they're just handing stuff out in the street.

Beat.

I need to know who they are. Can we, can we work together, on this?

Beat.

Nidal.

Nidal   Yes.

Bradley   I need to know who / they're working with. I have to write this up.

Nidal   Yes.

Bradley   When you identify these people you're going to liaise with me.

Nidal   Yes.

Bradley   I have to write a report on this. The Major wants a report on this. / I have to identify them, you understand what I'm saying?

Nidal   Yes.

Bradley *sees one of the* **IFP** *threatening one of the detainees.*

Bradley   I have to talk to the arresting officers. Who are they?

Nidal *shrugs.*

The **IFP** *continue to beat the detainees throughout the scene.*

Bradley   They don't look like fighters.

Nidal   Yes, they are insurgents.

Bradley   How old are they?

Nidal (*in Arabic*)   How old are you?

Detainee (*in Arabic*)   Forty-six.

Nidal   Four. Four-six.

Bradley   Forty-six.

Beat.

IFP (*in Arabic*)   *You will be punished for spreading lies!*

One of the **IFP** *strikes detainee.*

Bradley   Give me that – give me what they've got.

Nidal *hands over the literature.*

Bradley *takes it and walks to the* **Major***'s desk and stands at attention.*

Chorus *flocks in as* **Bradley***, but one by one they switch to stand with the* **Major***.*

Major   Specialist.

Bradley   Sir. I investigated the fifteen people arrested by the IFP on November 10th. The IFP claimed they were insurgents distributing anti-American literature and were part of a wider organisation.

Major   And?

Bradley   Sir, they're not insurgents.

Beat.

They're just. They're just protestors.

Major   I don't understand.

Bradley   This is the literature the IFP retrieved, I had it translated. It's not anti-American, sir. It's – you can read it for yourself. They're accusing the Iraqi government of corruption. They're accusing the Iraqi government of stealing aid.

Beat.

Major   Who authorised this translation?

Bradley   We're wasting our time on them, sir. They're not insurgents.

Major (*louder*)   Who authorised the translation?

Pause.

Bradley   I did, sir.

Silence.

I was using my initiative, sir.

Silence.

I had. I thought. I had suspicions that these weren't. They didn't look like insurgents, sir. I think. By doing this. I've, I've saved us resources so we don't spend time gathering intel on these fifteen / when, when they're just, regular –

Major (*loud*)   Your role is to support our brigades on the ground by identifying and tracking insurgents.

Bradley Yes, sir.

Major (*holding up the Iraqi translation literature*) How the hell does this support our brigades?

Silence.

Bradley I've stopped us wasting time gathering intel / on people who aren't the enemy.

Major How does *this* help support our brigade?

Silence.

Bradley I've saved resources, sir.

Major Do you have an attitude problem, Specialist?

Bradley Sir, no, sir.

Major Do you have a problem following orders, Specialist?

Bradley Sir, no, sir.

Major If the IFP says that's an insurgent, that's an insurgent. You do not spend time proving their innocence, you spend time finding more! Do you understand, Specialist? You want to show some initiative, come in here in two days' time, and say you've doubled the IFP haul, do I make myself clear?

Beat.

I want more / insurgents, not less!

Scene Twenty-Four

April 2010.

Tyler's *student house.*

Sound of mortar fire and **Chorus** *hits the floor. It could be a post-student house party. It could be dead Iraqi civilians. Some are dead, some are nearly dead.*

Bradley Security is a fucking joke.

He sits at a laptop. **Tyler** *stands behind him.*

Beat.

You forget your pass, you just knock on the door and someone lets you in. Passwords to every computer are on sticky notes pressed on to monitors. Why has no one leaked anything?

Beat.

Tyler   Sounds crazy.

Bradley   Did you read the 9/11 pagers released on WikiLeaks?

Tyler   Uh, no.

Bradley   That definitely came from someone in the NSA because I've read those on the inside.

Beat.

Tyler.

Tyler   What?

Bradley   They can't crack the encryption. Somebody leaked but the FBI can't figure out who. They've got no one. If WikiLeaks don't know who uploaded it, how can the FBI?

Tyler   Bradley –

Bradley   Do you know they brought gravel and pebbles from Turkey so that the KBR contractors don't get their feet too dirty when it rains?

Beat.

Man, I'm so glad to be out of that room, I thought I was going insane. Fourteen hours a day I'm looking at a screen, or sweeping the floor in the same room. Six days a week, I'm bombarded with all this information that no one's allowed to see, and I can see it, as long as I act like I don't care.

Beat.

I can read about plots to assassinate heads of state, but I can't tell anyone about *you*.

Tyler   Bradley, *listen*, the reason / why I said you needed to come over this weekend –

Bradley   Sorry, I haven't finished. I used to hack so that I could unlock myself and feel free. Now, I see all this stuff about torture and civilian deaths and *I'm* the security. It's the opposite of everything I believe in. I wish I hadn't seen half of it.

He looks at the dead bodies.

Yeah.

Beat.

Now I can't get it out of my mind.

Beat.

So. I'm thinking of leaking something myself.

Silence.

I've worked out how I can do it. It's simple I just take in a re-writable CD with something like Lady Gaga written on. Stick it in a machine, and then re-write with all the classified info and lip-synch while I drag and drop the shit out of those servers.

He laughs nervously.

Tyler   Okay, just stop / for a minute.

Bradley   There's a video. I just found it in a zip file.

Beat.

It's an Apache helicopter shooting civilians on the street with a thirty-millimetre cannon.

Beat.

And.

Beat.

I *can't* stop watching it.

Beat.

They circle them for a while.

Beat.

You'd think they'd all be looking up at the helicopter, but they can't see or hear it because the Apache's nearly a mile away. They fire and these people don't know where they're being shot at from. Some hide behind a wall, but because they can't see the helicopter they don't realise the helicopter can see them.

Beat.

One guy sort of just . . . explodes.

Beat.

And, I can't, stop, watching it. Nobody asks any questions if you're watching stuff like that because, everyone's watching videos like that.

Beat.

We're supposed to make sense of it.

Silence

All I can think . . . every time I watch it, I think . . .

Beat.

Maybe *this* time they'll get away.

Beat.

Tyler   Don't look at me. I don't know what you expect me to do with all this.

Beat.

Bradley   I can't be myself, because, if I try to be myself, I have to do something. The longer I'm there, the more I feel like I don't have a choice.

Beat.

I'm sorry I'm just . . . I need a drink or something.

Tyler *looks around the room – can he see the bodies that haunt* **Bradley***? Does a body reach out to* **Tyler** *for help?*

Tyler   I don't want you using all your leave to come see me.

Bradley (*flirty*)   Shut up.

Tyler   I don't want you using all your leave on me.

Bradley   I *want* to come see you.

Tyler   I know.

He backs away from the bodies.

I just think you should use your . . . Maybe some other folks would like to see you; I don't want to hog / you from your family.

Bradley   Who am I going to go and see? My dad?

Tyler   You know what / I'm saying.

Bradley   Being stupid, Tyler.

Tyler   I'm thinking of you.

Bradley   And I think of you every single second I'm in that box. I count down the hours till I can see you again.

Bradley *kisses* **Tyler**. **Tyler** *is non-committal.*

Tyler   I know.

Bradley *senses* **Tyler***'s distancing.*

Bradley   What?

Tyler   It's nothing.

Bradley   You're such a headfuck.

Tyler   I'm sorry.

He backs away from the bodies.

It's just. I've got finals coming up. You're a *soldier*.

Silence.

I'm just a student.

Beat.

We're just.

Beat.

I've got, finals coming up.

Scene Twenty-Five

May 2004.

Tasker Milward V C School.

Mrs Stokes   You've *all* got finals coming up. So today we're going to concentrate on Chartism and the Newport Rising. Lisa, stop talking.

Beat.

In 1839, the last armed rebellion against the government on mainland Britain descended on Newport. Who's John Frost, Gavin?

Gavin   Chartist, miss.

Mrs Stokes   Chartist leader, Gavin. He'd made more public speeches, written more pamphlets than anyone else. But now the rising was happening, he wasn't sure it was the right thing to do and he tried to persuade the workers to go back home but they refused. Mark, stop talking.

Beat.

So did John Frost turn his back on history and go back to writing and thinking about change? Or did he take action? Lisa?

Lisa   Um . . .

Mrs Stokes   What did John Frost do?

Lisa   Um . . . he like. Was he. / No, hang on. I know.

Mrs Stokes   Bradley, stand by the board and write the names of anyone who tries to talk while I'm talking. The last person on the board at the end of the class gets detention. You keep an eye on the class, in case I miss anyone.

Bradley *gets up picks up a piece of chalk.*

Mrs Stokes (*to* **Bradley**)   Lisa.

Bradley *writes 'Lisa' on the board.*

Mrs Stokes   He took action, and led the uprising. He was arrested and sent to Australia for his part. (*To* **Bradley**.) Gavin.

This time **Bradley** *takes his time writing 'Gavin'.*

Mrs Stokes   John Frost is one name in a long list of Welsh radicals. I want you to show wider reading in your exams, so you have a task. Go home and research on the internet the following people: Gwynfor Evans, James Keir Hardie, Tyrone O'Sullivan, the Women for Life on Earth, Aneurin Bevan. All these people found themselves at pivotal moments in history and had no choice but to act – such was the power of their convictions. Mark, are you chewing gum?

Mark   No, miss.

Mrs Stokes   Then you're talking. Bradley.

Bradley *doesn't respond.*

Mrs Stokes   Bradley, put Mark's name down.

Bradley *doesn't. He puts the chalk down and heads to his desk.*

Mrs Stokes   What are you doing, Bradley?

Bradley   I'm not putting anyone else's name on the board.

Mrs Stokes   Why not?

Bradley   I'm just not.

Beat.

Mrs Stokes   Fine I'll get someone / else to do it.

Bradley   I don't think anyone else should either.

Mrs Stokes   What do you mean by that?

Bradley   I don't think any of us should. We don't have to help you punish us.

He sits down.

Mrs Stokes   Lisa. Go to the front please, pick up some chalk. As I was saying, these figures in history –

Lisa *doesn't move.*

Mrs Stokes   Lisa.

Beat.

Go to the front.

Beat.

Gavin. Front of the class please. Pick up a piece of chalk.

Gavin   No, I'm alright here, miss, I want to get all this down.

Mrs Stokes   Mark? Front of the class.

Beat.

Mark   I've done it before, miss.

Mrs Stokes   I don't want to have to put you in detention. What's the matter with you?

Scene Twenty-Six

May 2010.

Forward Operating Base Hammer.

Bradley   If I knew I wouldn't be here.

Two **Bradleys**, *one male and one female, fighting in front of three* **Counsellors**. *Each* **Counsellor** *holds his/her hands in the 'See no evil, hear no evil, speak no evil' position. They are oblivious to the conflict between the two* **Bradleys** *over whose voice should be heard.*

Male and female **Bradleys** *struggle with each other.*

Deaf Counsellor   How is work?

Beat.

And your relationship?

Beat.

What do you want to talk about, Bradley?

Beat.

Blind Counsellor   This is your time.

Very long silence.

Bradley   You have no idea, what it's like trying to talk to you.

Deaf Counsellor   We're trained army therapists.

Beat.

We're experts with stress!

Pause.

Blind Counsellor   What's the first thing that comes to mind?

Silence.

Bradley   Command . . . asked me to look into . . . why, these two groups were meeting in Basra.

Beat.

Recommended a sourcing mission.

Beat.

Did not recommend: engagement.

Blind Counsellor   But they were engaged.

Silence.

Deaf Counsellor   What did the log say, was it enemy or friendly action?

Bradley   Log said enemy.

Silence.

Why would the CCIR warn against negative publicity?

Beat.

Why say that, if they were enemy kills?

Beat.

Blind Counsellor   You have to trust the OIC.

Bradley   I do.

Beat.

I don't know . . . what . . . they're dealing with.

Deaf Counsellor   Why is this troubling you?

Silence.

Bradley   I read: on my girlfriend's Facebook status . . . She now considers herself . . .

Beat.

Single.

Deaf Counsellor   Your relationship is over?

Mute Counsellor *gasps, everyone looks at him/her.*

Bradley   Not for, for me, seems that way for hi – her.

Blind Counsellor   How were things when you last saw her?

Very long silence.

Bradley   She's in Brandeis, so –

Beat.

Everyone.

Beat.

That's her status. Only it's patently not.

Beat.

There's someone halfway, halfway round the world in a warzone. Crying. I'm crying every night because I, because she, she won't reply to any messages.

Beat.

What he . . . What she's put. I want. I. Her relationship status is not true. It's not true. It might be what . . . she wants, but it's not that's not . . . how it is.

Beat.

I've.

Beat.

She's got all the . . .

Mute Counsellor *nods in understanding.*

Bradley   I can see how, someone . . . can try to just . . . wipe someone from existence. How can? How can someone just deny a year-long relationship ever existed . . . with a sentence?

Pause.

And . . . it's got me thinking, you know. About the logs. Why would we *ever* record a mistake?

Silence.

Blind Counsellor   Because we're the professionals.

Bradley   That gives us *every* reason not to record mistakes.

Mute Counsellor *shakes his/her head.*

Bradley   I. Some guy . . . left his house today, and four hundred clicks away I couldn't decide what his politics were from his fucking cell use, so he got shot in the head.

Beat.

You know, it's, it's just one. It's just one letter . . . on a, on a keypad. Add an E to the KIA and no one asks any questions. Enemy killed in action.

Beat.

The world can't be like this, or I can't be in it.

Scene Twenty-Seven

February 2011.

Quantico brig.

Bradley *makes sounds to re-acquaint himself with his voice.*

Bradley   I'M KINDA BUSY K-K-K KINDA BUSY.

Beat.

K-K-K-K-K-K-K-KINDA BUSY.

I-I-I-I-I-I'M KINDA CHAPTER FIFTEEN.

CH-CH-CH-CHAPTER FIFTEEN.

CHA-CHA-CHA!

He makes more sounds re-acquainting himself with his voice.

I-I-I-I-I-I-I-I-I-I-I-I-I –

Beat.

I missss.

Beat.

MMMMmmmmiiiissssssss –

I miss.

Beat.

I misssssssss –

Beat.

My mother.

He makes sounds.

Beat.

Gay.

Beat.

Chapter fifteen.

Beat.

Gay.

Beat.

G-uuhh –

Beat.

G-uuuuuuhhhh –

Beat.

G-uuuhhhaaaaayyyyy. Gay. Gay. Gay. Gay.

Maximum!

Beat.

Maximum.

Beat.

Maxi-mum.

Beat.

Maxi-mum. Maxinum. Mnaxinum. Aximum. Maxinum. Manaximum. Manningaximum. Manaxing. Man. Man. Mannnnnnning. Mannnnning. Manning.

Beat.

Manning. Mmm.

Beat.

MMMMmmmmmmmmm.

He makes sounds as if he's warming up his voice.

A meal slides out from under the door into the middle of the room.

FOOD! F-F-F-F-FOOOOOOOD. DUH. DUH. DUH. Beans!

Thanks!

Beat.

Thank you!

Beat.

Thank you for my food! Foood!

Silence.

Confronted with the silence, **Bradley** *turns to his food. He tries to eat but can't.*

He stares at the plate.

Beat.

He screams with frustration and hurls the plate and food against a wall.

As the plate hits the wall, a female **Chorus** *hits the floor.*

Scene Twenty-Eight

May 2010.

Forward Operating Base Hammer.

Chorus *stands as one with* **Commander**.

Commander   Specialist Manning, you have been reported for striking an officer!

Holding his gun, **Bradley** *stands before a* **Commander**. **Chorus** *bodies sprawl around.*

Commander   Do you have anything to say on the matter?

Bradley   No sir!

Commander   I am issuing you with Company Grade Article Fifteen; you will be reduced in rank to Private.

Beat.

Hand me your weapon.

Bradley   My weapon, sir?

Commander   Now, Manning.

Bradley *struggles to get his bolt out of his gun and places it on the desk.* **Commander** *takes the bolt and places it in his drawer. He stares at* **Bradley**. **Bradley** *looks straight ahead.*

Commander   Behavioural Health sent me your psych files.

He turns pages.

Anything you want to say, Private?

Long pause.

Bradley   No, sir.

Silence.

I thought . . . my medical files were, confidential, sir.

Commander *thumbs through the files.*

Commander   Anything else you want to say, Private?

Silence.

He turns a page.

Silence

He turns a page.

Silence.

He turns a page.

Silence.

He turns a page.

Silence.

He turns a page.

Bradley   Sir. Can I ask why you've removed my weapon?

Commander *turns a page.*

Commander   Because I have to ensure the safety of everyone on this base. Including yourself, Manning.

Bradley   I'm not a risk to myself or anyone else, sir.

Commander   I have a female sergeant with a bust lip that might disagree with you, Manning.

Silence.

He turns another page.

Silence.

The behavioural unit has put your actions down to 'adjustment disorder'.

Beat.

Your time at FOB Hammer is over. In three days time you will be back in Fort Leavenworth where the Discharge Unit will start to process you and end your military service.

Beat.

I want you take the last few days of your security clearance to finish any unwritten reports, liaise with Specialist Marino so we have continuity with briefings, then you will be assigned to the Supply Office while you wait for redeployment to the States. Your discharge cannot jeopardise any ongoing operations. The war is over / for you, Manning.

Bradley   Sir, I lost my temper, but I still have a lot to offer the Brigade.

Commander (*reading*)   'The persona I'm forced to take on, is killing the fuck out of me.'

Bradley (*rising*)   Sir, I understood my counselling to be confidential.

Commander (*rising*)   'I don't know, I think I'm weird, I guess. I can't separate myself from others. I feel connected to everybody, like they were a distant family.'

Bradley (*rising*)   Sir, that's . . .

Commander   'Specialist Manning recalled dressing as a woman while on leave.'

Bradley (*rising*)   THAT IS NOT YOUR BUS / INESS.

Commander   IT IS MY BUSINESS BECAUSE I DON'T TRUST / YOU.

Bradley   AND I DON'T TRUST YOU! I'M NOT A FUCKING PIECE OF EQUIPMENT!

Commander   YOUR CAREER IS OVER, MANNING. AND SO IS YOUR WAR. DISMISSED.

Bradley *turns.*

Commander   Salute your superior officer.

As **Bradley** *slowly obeys, he underscores the salute with a defiance suggesting this is his final act of personal betrayal and military loyalty..*

Scene Twenty-Nine

May 2010.

Forward Operating Base Hammer, Eastern Baghdad.

Intel Officer 2   Hey, Manning, I've sent you the video of the Hellfire taking a guy's head off.

Bradley *stands in the Intel room.*

Intel Officers *sit around, as usual chewing gum, watching videos, listening to music and throwing stress balls around.*

Bradley   Great.

Intel Officer 2   Boom!

Bradley *sits at a computer console.*

The rest of the department go about their business. Passing files around, logging reports. Answering phones, working on computers.

Trying to hide his fears, **Bradley** *looks around the room.*

He takes a deep, long breath.

Pause.

Professionally, **Bradley** *goes to his bag and gets a CD out. He puts headphones on.*

He puts a CD into a computer and starts to mine the data and transfer it to his CD.

Quietly, **Bradley** *starts mouthing the words to Lady Gaga's 'Born This Way'.*

As **Bradley** *sings 'Born This Way', we begin to hear it.*

As we hear the music, so do the **Intel Officers/Chorus***. One by one the* **Chorus** *gets overcome by the music and breaks into a dance conflating the sentiment of the song and their military personas.*

As **Bradley** *completes the download, the* **Chorus** *starts hungrily to pull paperwork from his hands, much to his delight.*

The 'Gaga army' distributes secret embassy cables and war logs from the Afghan and Iraq wars to the audience, with abandon.

Bradley *hurls cables into the air.*

The sequence concludes when every **Chorus** *member is* **Bradley**.

Scene Thirty

March 2011.

Bradley *in Quantico brig.*

He breaks down as he is tortured with repetitive questioning.

Marine 1   Detainee 4335453, are you okay?

Bradley   Yes.

Marine 1   Detainee 4335453, are you okay?

Bradley   Yes.

Marine 1   Detainee 4335453, are you okay?

Bradley   Yes.

Marine 1   Detainee 4335453, are you okay?

Bradley   Yes. I'm fine.

Marine 1   Detainee 4335453, are you okay?

Bradley   Yes.

Marine 1   Detainee 4335453, are you okay?

Bradley   Yes.

Marine 1   Detainee 4335453, are you okay?

Bradley   Yes.

Marine 1   Detainee 4335453, are you okay?

Bradley   Yes. We don't have to do this every five minutes.

Marine 1   Detainee 4335453, are you okay?

Bradley   Yes.

Marine 1   Detainee 4335453, are you okay?

Bradley   Yes.

Marine 1   Detainee 4335453, are you okay?

Bradley   Yes.

Marine 1   Detainee 4335453, are you okay?

Bradley   Yes.

Marine 1   Detainee 4335453, are you okay?

Bradley   Yes.

Marine 1   Detainee 4335453, are you okay?

Bradley   Yes.

Marine 1   Detainee 4335453, are you okay?

Bradley   Yes.

Marine 1   Detainee 4335453, are you okay?

Bradley   Yes.

Marine 1   Detainee 4335453, are you okay?

Bradley   Yes.

Marine 1   Detainee 4335453, are you okay?

Bradley   Yes.

Marine 1   Detainee 4335453, are you okay?

Bradley   Yes.

Marine 1   Detainee 4335453, are you okay?

Bradley   Yes.

Marine 1   Detainee 4335453, are you okay?

Bradley   Yes.

Marine 1   Detainee 4335453, are you okay?

Bradley   Yes.

Marine 1   Detainee 4335453, are you okay?

Bradley   Yes. I'm not a risk to myself.

Marine 1   Detainee 4335453, are you okay?

Bradley   Yes.

Marine 1   Detainee 4335453, are you okay?

Bradley   Yes.

Marine 1   Detainee 4335453, are you okay?

Bradley   Yes.

Marine 1   Detainee 4335453, are you okay?

Bradley   Yes.

Marine 1   Detainee 4335453, are you okay?

Bradley   Yes.

Marine 1   Detainee 4335453, are you okay?

Bradley   Yes.

Marine 1   Detainee 4335453, are you okay?

Bradley   Yes.

Marine 1   Detainee 4335453, are you okay?

Bradley   Yes.

Marine 1   Detainee 4335453, are you okay?

Bradley   Yes.

Marine 1   Detainee 4335453, are you okay?

Bradley   Yes.

Marine 1   Detainee 4335453, are you okay?

Bradley   Yes.

Marine 1   Detainee 4335453, are you okay?

Bradley   Yes.

Marine 1   Detainee 4335453, are you okay?

Bradley   Yes.

Marine 1   Detainee 4335453, are you okay?

Bradley   Yes.

Marine 1   Detainee 4335453, are you okay?

Bradley   Yes.

Marine 1   Detainee 4335453, are you okay?

Bradley   Yes.

Marine 1   Detainee 4335453, are you okay?

Bradley   Yes.

Marine 1   Detainee 4335453, are you okay?

Bradley   Yes.

Marine 1   Detainee 4335453, are you okay?

Bradley   Yes.

Marine 1   Detainee 4335453, are you okay?

Bradley   Yes.

Marine 1   Detainee 4335453, are you okay?

Bradley   Yes.

Marine 1   Detainee 4335453, are you okay?

Bradley *gathers himself.*

Bradley   Yes.

Marine 1   Detainee 4335453, are you okay?

Bradley *stands up and stands to attention.*

Bradley   Yes.

Marine 1   Detainee 4335453, are you okay?

Bradley   Yes.

Marine 1   Detainee 4335453, are you okay?

Bradley   Yes.

Scene Thirty-One

May 2004.

Tasker Milward V C School.

Mrs Stokes   Detention over!

Class *bursts out of its chairs.*

Except you, Bradley.

He sits back down. They are alone.

Do you like it here?

He shrugs.

Think you might stay here?

Bradley   I don't know.

Silence.

Mrs Stokes   I thought you were going to try and take a deep breath for me before opening your mouth and getting into trouble.

Bradley   I kept my promise.

Mrs Stokes   So why did I just have a whole class revolting against me?

Bradley   I did what you / said.

Mrs Stokes   No you didn't, you got into an argument like you always do.

Bradley   No, I did what you said.

Beat.

Mrs Stokes   And?

Bradley   It worked. I got clarity.

Silence.

Mrs Stokes   I don't know how your mam copes with you.

He shrugs.

Bradley   I'm sort of. Taking care of her.

Beat.

Me and Anthony, we've built this website, it's sort of like a news aggregator, and social network for the county. People can come and post local news and stuff. Hoping that'll take off.

Beat.

We need the money.

Mrs Stokes   Is that what you'd like to do? Run something like Apple?

Silence.

Bradley   I don't know.

Beat.

I'm smart, I can do stuff. But I want to use it to help people. I see all these people walking around and. None of them know how much I can help them.

Mrs Stokes   That's very noble. I don't hear many boys your age talk about a desire to serve their community.

Beat.

Bradley   I guess that's why I think I'll probably join the US Army.

Mrs Stokes   Why's that?

Bradley   We have to protect our country. I love America.

Beat.

Mrs Stokes   Don't you love Wales?

Bradley   Yeah. But.

Beat.

If I want to make help people, make the world a better place I can't think of anywhere better than the US Army.

Mrs Stokes   I don't want you to join the army.

Beat.

Bradley   I don't have a choice, miss.

Lights down.